The Complete Guide to

Pruning Trees and Bushes

Everything You Need to
Know Explained Simply

K.O. Morgan

The Complete Guide to Pruning Trees and Bushes
Everything You Need to Know Explained Simply

Library of Congress Cataloging-in-Publication Data

Morgan, K. O. (Kim O.), 1957-
 The complete guide to pruning trees and bushes : everything you need to know explained simply / by: K.O. Morgan.
    p. cm.
 Includes bibliographical references and index.
 ISBN-13: 978-1-60138-344-0 (alk. paper)
 ISBN-10: 1-60138-344-4 (alk. paper)
 1. Trees--Pruning. 2. Shrubs--Pruning. I. Title.
 SD407.M67 2010
 635.9'77--dc22
                          2010041207

PROJECT MANAGER: Shannon McCarthy
BOOK PRODUCTION DESIGN: T.L. Price • design@tlpricefreelance.com
COVER DESIGN: Meg Buchner • megadesn@mchsi.com
BACK COVER DESIGN: Jackie Miller • millerjackiej@gmail.com

Printed in the United States

Printed on Recycled Paper

We recently lost our beloved pet "Bear," who was not only our best and dearest friend but also the "Vice President of Sunshine" here at Atlantic Publishing. He did not receive a salary but worked tirelessly 24 hours a day to please his parents. Bear was a rescue dog that turned around and showered myself, my wife, Sherri, his grandparents Jean, Bob, and Nancy, and every person and animal he met (maybe not rabbits) with friendship and love. He made a lot of people smile every day.

We wanted you to know that a portion of the profits of this book will be donated to The Humane Society of the United States. *–Douglas & Sherri Brown*

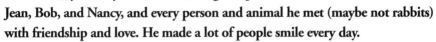

The human-animal bond is as old as human history. We cherish our animal companions for their unconditional affection and acceptance. We feel a thrill when we glimpse wild creatures in their natural habitat or in our own backyard.

Unfortunately, the human-animal bond has at times been weakened. Humans have exploited some animal species to the point of extinction.

The Humane Society of the United States makes a difference in the lives of animals here at home and worldwide. The HSUS is dedicated to creating a world where our relationship with animals is guided by compassion. We seek a truly humane society in which animals are respected for their intrinsic value, and where the human-animal bond is strong.

Want to help animals? We have plenty of suggestions. Adopt a pet from a local shelter, join The Humane Society and be a part of our work to help companion animals and wildlife. You will be funding our educational, legislative, investigative and outreach projects in the U.S. and across the globe.

Or perhaps you'd like to make a memorial donation in honor of a pet, friend or relative? You can through our Kindred Spirits program. And if you'd like to contribute in a more structured way, our Planned Giving Office has suggestions about estate planning, annuities, and even gifts of stock that avoid capital gains taxes.

Maybe you have land that you would like to preserve as a lasting habitat for wildlife. Our Wildlife Land Trust can help you. Perhaps the land you want to share is a backyard—that's enough. Our Urban Wildlife Sanctuary Program will show you how to create a habitat for your wild neighbors.

So you see, it's easy to help animals. And The HSUS is here to help.

THE HUMANE SOCIETY
OF THE UNITED STATES.

2100 L Street NW • Washington, DC 20037 • 202-452-1100
www.hsus.org

Author dedication

This book is dedicated to my late father, Kenneth B. Morgan, who did *not* have a green thumb but admired those who do.

Table of Contents

Chapter 3: Safety First 39

Chapter 4: The Right Tool for the Job 47

Chapter 5: General Pruning Rules 61

Chapter 6: Common Pruning Methods 85

Chapter 7: Other Pruning Methods 99

Chapter 8: Pruning Deciduous Trees 151

Chapter 9: Pruning Popular Fruit Trees........................157

Conclusion 263

Appendix A: Recognizing Hazardous Defects in Trees 265

Introduction

Pruning is the act of clearing excess vegetation from a plant to remove diseased tissue, reinvigorate growth, increase fruit or nut production, or optimize the space the plant occupies. Some people strongly believe that plants should grow naturally because nature takes care of any problems that could occur along the way. Also, some organic purists think crop-producing trees should grow freely without ever seeing the sharp blade of a pruning tool. On the surface, this philosophy makes sense: Trees and plants growing wildly in our forests seem perfectly healthy to a casual observer whizzing by in a car at 60 mph. But, take a closer look at forest growth. You will first notice on closer observation the major battle going on in the forest for space and light. Fast-growing, invasive trees stemming from seed-infested bird droppings create life-sapping shade as they steal nutrients and moisture from the root systems of century-old oaks. Huge limbs damaged from insects, wind, and ice storms dangle from trees, threatening plants below. Dead limbs that harbor termites and other insects that can move into living trees, eventually killing them, litter the forest floor. Dead branches that hang low to the ground and shade out broad-leafed herbs called forbs and grasses, which provide valuable wildlife food, restrict the movement of large animals. To make matters worse, imported garden plants that wildlife cannot eat have escaped cultivation and have sprouted up everywhere.

The typical North American forest became such an unnatural, unproductive place because fire — a natural cleansing agent that kills invasive plants, cleans the forest floor, and naturally prunes the lower limbs of trees — is no longer part of the forest life cycle because when fire naturally appears, it is quickly suppressed. Fire possibly provided the pruning agent for forests. Because fire is no longer, or rarely, a part of the forest experience in North America, particularly in areas where human populations live close by, man must remove or prune overgrowth, undergrowth, and invasive species. In many cases, this is done through controlled burns, a method of forest management often used in federally and state-owned land in which forest management agencies use naturally occurring fires from lightning or dry vegetation that ignites and then control the burn through weather conditions and fire-management techniques. This ensures that the fire does not threaten wildlife, nearby human populations, or the entire forest vegetation itself. Controlled burns can also be prescribed fires in which management agencies start the fires themselves as a way to improve the forest and grassland health. Forests not government-owned or under some kind of management are often not healthy forest systems.

Now, take this argument a step further, and look at a typical ornamental landscape. You obviously cannot set fire to it to clean it up so man must remove diseased limbs and overgrowth that prevent air circulation and access to extend the lives of trees and bushes and create a sense of balance. People must manage native plants, as well as fast-growing, non-native plants, or they will try to take over all available space in the garden. For example, while there are native fruit trees, such as the wild plum or apple, all fruit trees that produce grocery-store-quality produce are cultivars. Cultivars are fruit trees specifically selected and cultivated for certain characteristics, such as the desired crop yield or resistance to diseases, which cannot be left alone in the garden year after year. Every fruit tree grower would love to find a variety of peach, apple, or plum tree that would live more than 10 years and produce endless beautiful fruit every year without the need for pruning or spraying with insecticides, but those types of improved fruit trees simply do not exist.

You can see how important pruning is to landscape and plant management. Without it, the beautiful garden you visualize when you close your eyes could not exist, and the open forest full of wildlife and native plants would be overgrown and full of damaged and diseased wood. The bushels of huge, sweet fruit would not be available in grocery stores, and the beautiful and fragrant flowers from the florist would be small and less vibrant. If these reasons do not convince you of the importance of pruning, just remember how overgrown and unsightly every lawn would be without a pruning program — after all, cutting the grass is the most common form of pruning done in the United States.

Overview of This Book

The Complete Guide to Pruning Trees and Bushes: Everything You Need to Know Explained Simply aims to help the average person understand when the pruning of trees and bushes, also known as shrubs, is needed, as well as the correct way to prune and how to use the correct tools. This book discusses different types of pruning, including several rare and artistic methods, in an easy-to-understand format.

The book begins by discussing the difference between a bush and a tree and by detailing the different structures of each. This anatomy is clearly explained so the reader can understand how pruning affects the health of the plant and how a plant heals after pruning. Because establishing a need for pruning is the first step in the pruning process, this book also discusses the reasons for pruning. It also includes a list of the tools needed to complete a specific job, along with an overview of the correct way to use different pruning tools.

Detailed information is given about the different ways of pruning a variety of trees and bushes, from cutting large limbs from the tallest trees to correcting storm damage to pinching the stem ends of perennials shrubs to create a bushier growth habit. **Deciduous**, or leaf-dropping, trees and shrubs and evergreen trees, which do not lose their leaves in winter, along with fruit and nut trees, are all provided in a special section because you prune and maintain them differently. Another section is devoted to roses because pruning is an integral part of caring for roses. Descriptions of certain trees or shrubs include that tree or shrub's ability to survive in certain USDA horticultural zones that are based on average annual minimum temperatures for each zone.

This book is designed as a field manual on pruning for both amateurs and professionals. It includes an easy-to-understand index and chapter headings to help you quickly locate the type of plant you are pruning, along with a detailed description of each pruning procedure. For example, under the fruit tree section in the index, the most common fruit trees grown in the United States and the correct pruning method for each are clearly marked and explained in detail.

After reading this book, the reader should be able to confidently and effectively prune a tree or shrub throughout the life of that individual tree or shrub. While ease of pruning will come with experience, this book will serve as the go-to book for amateur and professional gardeners alike.

Chapter 1:

Anatomy of a Tree and a Bush

Certain characteristics make a tree, a tree and a bush, a bush. A **tree** is a perennial plant with a distinct woody main trunk and a series of branches growing from the main trunk. In addition, a tree's branches form a **crown**, which is where the leaf and branch structures are located and what gives the tree its shape. It defines a tree and should be unaltered to allow the tree to form a natural shape. A tree also has an average height of 15 feet. A **bush** — or shrub as it is also known — does not have a main trunk and consists of a series of smaller branches that grow from the **root crown**. This is the transitional area at the surface of the soil where the roots turn into woody stems as they grow from the ground. *Note: You should not confuse a tree with a bush pruned to resemble a tree.*

The limbs and main trunk of a tree or bush serve two purposes: First, naturally structured limbs create an efficient circulatory system for the plant to transport water and nutrients from the roots of the plant to the leaves. Then, the limbs and main trunk hold the leaves at an optimal position to receive maximum exposure to light so that photosynthesis can occur. **Photosynthesis** is the process where the plant uses sunlight shining on the leaves to create a simple sugar to use as food and energy. This energy is then delivered down to the roots.

Removing too many leaves and limbs from a tree or shrub, so that it cannot produce enough energy to survive, can result in plant shock or death. That is why pruning is often done in stages, sometimes a year or more apart, so the plant has time to recover or heal between each pruning session.

The circulatory system of the plant depends on a process called transpiration because plants do not have a heart to pump water and nutrients from one area to another. **Transpiration** occurs as water evaporates from the pores in the undersides of leaves. As the water is pulled from the plant into the atmosphere, it moves from the roots of the plants to replace what is lost in the leaf structure. Some of the water is converted to sugar through photosynthesis and returned to the roots. The excess water is released through transpiration. A healthy and viable root system is just as important for the transpiration process to occur as a healthy **crown**, which is made up of all the limbs and leaves growing above ground. But, if there is too much top growth for the root system to support — because of low moisture levels in the soil, destruction of the roots by mechanical means, or root damage from disease or animals — the plant can suffer or die. This explains why pruning is often done to balance the amount of leaves or top growth with the available root system. Pruning done after someone moves a plant from one place to another, damaging roots in the process, provides on example of this.

Next is the internal part of a tree or branch. The rough brown or gray outer layer, known as the **bark,** covers the internal parts of the tree. The bark protects the tree from temperature extremes and also provides protection from insects and animals that can bore into the tree and disrupt the transpiration process. In young trees, you may only notice it as a smooth green or gray outer layer. Under the bark is the **cork cambium**, the layer of cells responsible for creating new bark. As the tree ages, the bark cells created by the cork cambium accumulate on the outside of the limbs and trunk and make the thick brown or gray corky layer recognized as the bark. A new layer of bark cells is created each year, creating a new ring — you can tell the age of a tree by simply counting the rings visible on a freshly cut stump. The next layer behind the cork cambium is the **phloem**, the layer of cells that conducts food from the leaves and moves it to areas of the plant that need food, often the roots. Behind the phloem is a thin layer of active tissue that produces new phloem cells on one side and new xylem cells on the other. It is known as the **cambium** layer.

The **xylem** is the entire inner part of the woody structure located behind the cambium layer; it is the supporting and water-conducting tissue of the plant. It can be separated into two sections: the sapwood and the heartwood. The **sapwood** is the place water and nutrients flow upward to the top of the tree or shrub during the transpiration process. The **heartwood** is the innermost layer and is dead tissue, but trees and shrubs depend on the strength of the heartwood for support as the tree ages. Most young trees or shrubs and their branches do not have an established layer of heartwood. Also, fast-growing trees, such as willows and some poplars, do not produce a thick or strong layer of heartwood, causing the limbs to break easily during ice and windstorms.

How a Plant Heals after Pruning

When a wound occurs on a large woody plant — and pruning is considered wounding the plant — the sapwood continues to send **sap** — a combination of water, nutrients, and sugar — toward the damaged area. The sap flows over the cut area and dries. The dried sap creates a barrier to protect the wound from common insects and disease. That is why the best place to cut a limb is near the main stem or trunk where there is a **branch collar**, an area that has robust cellular activity with strong sap flow and can, therefore, heal quickly and easily from mechanical damage. Also, the branch collar is located at an angle where water cannot collect and allow decay to establish.

For this reason, pruning must occur just outside the branch collar. Pruning flush against the trunk or main limb and cutting off the thick branch collar will damage the long-term health of the tree, allowing disease and insects to enter the main stem. If you prune by cutting somewhere along the branch instead of just outside the branch collar, the newly exposed end of the branch cannot heal properly and will begin to rot. The decay can spread down the limb past the collar and into the tree. Not until the limb completely decays and falls off can the root collar do its job of sealing off the wound. As you can tell, incorrect pruning is not conducive to the long-term health of trees and shrubs.

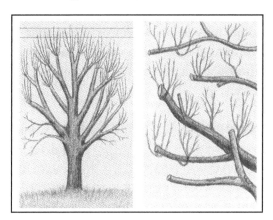

Left: Topping. Right: Tipping. Image courtesy of the USDA.

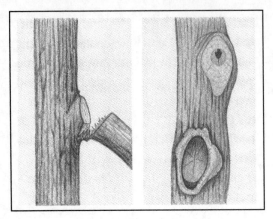

Left: Bark ripping. Right: Flesh cutting.
Image courtesy of the USDA.

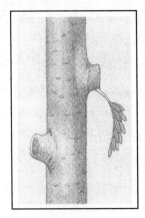

Stab cutting. Image
courtesy of the USDA.

In situations where you cannot cut entire branches, such as fruit trees and rose bushes, you should make a cut a ¼ inch above a leaf bud or leaf node growing in the desired direction, and you should make the cut at a slight angle with the top of the angle on the side of the cut that is away from center of the plant. This encourages new growth from the leaf bud in the desired direction, and the slight angle cut allows water to run off the damaged area. A branch cut in this manner heals at the leaf node where increased cellular activity helps seal the area for protection from insects and disease.

Chapter 2:

When and Why Do You Prune?

In nature, pruning occurs naturally, depending on the weather and wind conditions. Some trees, such as the silver maple and boxelder, naturally drop their branches no matter what the size, and others, such as persimmon trees, naturally shed twiggy branches after bearing fruit. Animals, such as deer and rabbits, prune trees and bushes. Deer enjoy eating the branches off trees, and rabbits will feast on suckers around the root bases of trees. In addition, lower tree and shrub branches often fall off because of lack of light. But nature's method of pruning is not always beneficial; wounds left from branches broken off in storms can lead to infection and disease, and sometimes new plants steal important nutrients from the soil of older trees, killing the older trees in the process.

Many people feel as if pruning interferes with nature, but with trees and shrubs grown in our gardens and yards, pruning often becomes important and necessary. Many reasons to prune exist: to make a plant more attractive; to create an artistic display; to improve the plant's health by making sure the lower limbs receive adequate light and dead branches do not encourage insect infestation and disease; to ensure safety for you, your family, and your neighbors; and to encourage new growth. Man-made pruning makes trees and shrubs more attractive and helps control their growth. You may not associate pruning with safety reasons, but these situations occur often, such as when a branch blocks your vision when backing out of your driveway or when a tree grows into power lines. When pruning for the right reasons and when performed correctly with the proper tools, pruning strengthens your trees and bushes.

Prune for safety. Image courtesy of the USDA.

Prune for health. Image courtesy of the USDA.

Prune for aesthetics. Image courtesy of the USDA.

You should always prune with purpose and not prune blindly. This means educating yourself about the correct tools to use for the plant you are pruning and to do so at the correct time of year or stage of the plant's growth. This book explores these issues because each species and variety requires a different pruning approach.

A note about auxin

Auxin represents a group of chemical compounds concentrated and produced in the tip end of the stems of a plant. These chemical compounds cause the cells in the tip end to elongate and multiply, producing what we normally define as plant growth. If you cut the tip end, you remove the main auxin-producing area. This signals the next bud in line to pick up the slack in auxin production. When you cut back the stem at an angle just above a leaf node or bud, you increase the chance that the auxin production will move to the bud located on the high end of the angle. When this happens, the end bud soon becomes the dominant and more vigorous bud.

Because auxin helps cells stretch or elongate, it plays an important role in helping plants move toward the light. When a part of a plant is shaded, the auxin moves to the shaded area of the plant, causing the shaded cells to become longer. As the cells in the shaded part of the plant "stretch," the plant is able to move toward the light.

You cannot overlook auxin's importance in all aspects of pruning. Effective pruning involves knowing how to manipulate auxin levels to create a desired outcome. For example, when you cut the end of one stem, you must accurately predict the location of the next auxin-producing area; in other words, you must study the stem and decide which bud you want to become the dominant bud and proceed to cut back the stem just above the bud. Once you know this, you can visualize where the new growth will come from and how the plant will look after new growth appears.

Fruit and Flower Production

People prune trees to encourage fruit production on fruit trees and flower production on perennials. Some fruit trees, such as peach trees, produce fruit on 1-year-old wood and require pruning often to encourage productive new growth in a structured way. Peach trees have a short life and are prone to **borers** — bugs that feed on the wood of trees — and other insect problems that attack unhealthy, old, or weak growth. Pruning removes these potential problems and forces the plant to concentrate its growing energy into

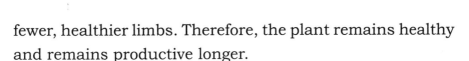

fewer, healthier limbs. Therefore, the plant remains healthy and remains productive longer.

Pruning can also prevent trees from blooming until they have become strong enough to bear fruit. Some fruit trees, like the pear tree, take years to bear fruit. Certain fruit trees will not bloom until they are 2 to 12 years old, depending on the kind of fruit tree. If a fruit tree produces fruit when it is too small, it may weaken the tree and prevent it from bearing fruit again for years. Therefore, you should cut off the first blooms or small fruits in order to prevent this from happening.

To continue with the example, look at some of the other problems that occur when a peach tree is never pruned and left to its own devices. A peach tree grows naturally straight up instead of into a broad, open shape, and any fruit produced is soon out of reach. As the peach tree grows out of control, numerous limbs begin crossing each other and shading out new growth. The dense growth in the tree's canopy prevents good air circulation and encourages fungus and mildew. Peach trees tend to produce fruit in clusters, and as it produces more peaches on the excessive new growth, the fruit becomes smaller and the crops become sporadic. During some years, the tree will have a heavy fruit load and other times light. In the years where the fruit load is heavy, the excess weight can break limbs, increasing the chance that insects and disease enter the tree through the damaged areas. Proper pruning keeps the fruit in easy reach and focuses the tree's energy to fewer peaches that grow much larger and sweeter. You can predict the crop more easily from year to year, and the tree remains healthy since you can easily notice disease and insect problems because excessive growth no longer hides them from view. As you can see, pruning a peach tree correctly creates a much better outcome.

Perennials, which are plants that can survive winter outdoors and bloom in the spring, such as hydrangeas, and which bloom on **new wood** — the wood produced during the current season — are often managed with the same philosophy as the peach tree. If the plant is managed in a way that produces fewer new limbs, then the plant produces larger blooms. Commercial cut flower growers, such as florists, retailers, brokers, and farmers, frequently manage blooming perennials so they produce flowers larger than average. If the plant is cut back in a way that allows the plant to grow many new branches, more blooms are produced, although they may be smaller. If you want to create larger blooms, such as those found in florist shops, you will need to remove new shoots. This way, you divert the plant's energy into fewer growing points, resulting in larger blooms. A plant that has not had its shoots pruned will be bushier with smaller flowers. Once the flowers are spent, you will then need to remove them, a process called **deadheading**, so you direct the plant's energy into making more blooms rather than seeds. This will keep your perennial energetic, and you may even get a second crop of flowers as a result.

Plants Affect Other Plant Growth

A managed landscape often has plants of all sizes that include trees, shrubs, bedding plants, and a lawn. Just as you cannot allow the lawn to grow out of control and crowd out the bedding plants, you cannot allow the woody plants to overwhelm or shade out other plants. You can clean a fast-growing tree, such as an ash, that produces many fast-growing, small branches within the canopy by properly removing the small branches. This allows more sunlight to shine through the canopy and reach the grassy areas, thus creating a healthier lawn because heavily shaded turf grass grows poorly and is susceptible to a variety of fungal and mildew diseases. You will have a healthier lawn, and plants that add color to the landscape can also thrive in the new sunny area.

This ornate garden has highly groomed hedges, a manicured lawn, and beautiful flowers.

Many plants are considered good candidates for hedges, and pruning aids in this effort, too. For example, Leyland cypresses — which can grow up to 3 feet a year — can quickly become large trees if not pruned on a regular basis. They can also shade out other plant growth, or the excessive shade may interfere with the neighbor's garden if allowed to grow too large. When this happens, you cannot prune the plants in a way that immediately creates a thick, attractive hedge. Or say you use a shrub as a hedge, but it has dramatically overgrown its bounds; if so, you must cut it back a little at a time, a process that may take several years. In either case, if the plants are suddenly pruned too severely, they may go into shock and die, creating more of an eyesore that is also expensive to remove.

Removing dead or diseased wood

Whether you are pruning a tree, shrub, woody perennial, rose bush, or fruit and nut tree, you need to remove dead or diseased wood during the process. One line of thought is that natural pruning occurs in nature when wind or ice breaks off dead and diseased limbs so one should wait for nature to takes its course. But, in a managed landscape, you cannot wait for this to happen. Broken limbs littering the landscape are unsightly and a fatal disease can spread throughout a plant or an entire crop of fruit trees after getting its start from one plant or tree with a damaged area. In addition, the dead or dying branches cause poor air circulation throughout the plant and can create moist conditions that promote the growth of disease-carrying organisms. Pruning these dead or dying limbs lets in more light that discourages the growth of these organisms. Therefore, it is imperative that you consistently look for dead or diseased wood on your plants and remove the wood immediately. The signs of disease will vary depending on the plant, but some common signs include discolored or falling leaves, sticky substances leaking from the tree, signs of hollowing of the trunk, limbs of a grey-brown color, and new growths around the roots. Once removed, throw all dead branches in a trash bag, and wash your pruning tools to prevent the spread of organisms, insects, and disease to other trees and shrubs in your yard.

Blocking pedestrian or vehicular traffic

If you have a house accessible by a walkway or driveway, or if it has sidewalks around it, you must control the plants that obstruct pedestrian and vehicular traffic. For example, if you live on a corner and your plants block the view of oncoming traffic or a stop sign, you could be held liable for a traffic accident that occurs because of the blocked line of sight. If the city decides to send someone to cut the tree or shrubs to create better visibility of the intersection or traffic sign, the chance of getting a professional pruning job is not good. The city will cut the offending plants more than what is needed, and you may also get the bill for the work done.

Having a hazard

Occasionally, a plant located around a house or another structure grows too large and creates places for wild animals — or even people — to hide. This creates a security issue, and it also decreases the air circulation around the structure, leading to mildew and mold problems on painted wood, brick, and stone. You must reduce the size of plants that grow too large and too close to your house or garage. You should prune them to an attractive shape, bringing them into balance with the rest of the landscape.

A limb from a large tree can weigh up to 1 ton or more, and you must remove limbs reaching out over the roof of a structure for safety's sake. If the limb is dead or diseased, you have even more of a reason to remove it before it falls. Good candidates for removal include large limbs that can fall over a long driveway and block vehicle access, as well as any dead or diseased limbs located over an area where children play. For your own safety, you should hire a professional arborist to prune large limbs and limbs high up on the tree. Trying to handle weighty tree limbs on your own or losing your balance on a tall ladder could result in injury or even death. Costs for professional arborists and tree pruners can vary, depending on the work involved and where you live.

Training the Plant into a Specific Shape

You can prune a shrub or tree to create a specific shape that pleases the eye or goes along with your landscape theme. The theme is chosen according to personal preference and can be functional, creative, or both. For example, you can tightly prune a row of bushes into a hedge that is flat across the top and sides. You can prune the same type of shrub into a hedge with a rounded shape if you live in an area that receives heavy snowfall. This prohibits the heavy snow from piling up and breaking the small limbs of the shrub, creating gaps in the hedge that you will see when the snow melts in the spring. You can prune a small tree or large shrub to have a bare trunk and a flat top so it looks like a giant mushroom, or you can prune boxwood into the shape of an animal. If you have the right plant and the right tools, you can prune plants into incredible shapes limited only by your imagination.

CASE STUDY: A PROFESSIONAL DECIDES WHEN TO PRUNE

Steve Pirus is a WSU Master Gardener and Certified Arborist in Vancouver, Washington, and a member of the International Society of Arboriculture.

We prune both to create a beautiful plant or tree and to maintain a healthy plant or tree. An arborist is actually a tree preservationist who puts the emphasis on plant health, and the artistic outcome just happens to come along with it. Typically, people choose to prune when they see a problem, meaning they visually do not like what the tree is doing or "looks" like. A knowledgeable gardener understands plant health and the reasons to prune and plans ahead, minimizing problems. It is proactive versus reactive.

First, we prune to remove any dead, dying, or diseased material — the three Ds. Next, remove any crossed branches; branches growing to the right of center should go out to the right, and branches to the left of center should go left. Otherwise the branches are competing with each other, wasting time and energy. Then, we remove suckers and water sprouts growing upright, usually straight, vertical branches.

The most common reasons for pruning would be the foliage is too low so we lift the skirt or crown. The standard height for doing this for public parks and sidewalks is 8 feet high, above the eyeballs of pedestrians, fast-running sports participants, and easy-target lawsuits. The homeowner would be well advised to plan this before power mowing and knocking his or her head.

Also view the clearing to see if foliage blocks a stop sign, the corner of an intersection, or the view of a river or ocean. Also remove any branches growing near the house exterior and banging in the wind, threatening damage to your property. Removing the limb is a much more cost-effective alternative to damaging your house.

You can also thin a tree's crown to help prevent power failure during high winds, removing about 25 to 30 percent of the foliage at any one time but not more. If you remove too much foliage, the tree often responds to the cuts by sending up fast, new, weak sprouts rather than slower, normal, more woody growth. So know this and do not get too carried away.

You should note that an arborist never, ever tops a tree. Topping, or hard-heading back, is reducing the size of the crown or greatly reducing the diameter of the tree. It encourages decay or dying back of the cuts, which can eventually die back into the trunk, slowly killing the tree.

We also do not cut a branch without a reason. Know what and why ahead of time. With plant health being foremost on the list, always use clean, sharp tools. Why clean? You would not go to a doctor who did not use clean, sterilized tools, and yet people will let sap and gum build up on their tools for weeks, months, and years. We first clean off the old sap with water, a cleanser, and a scouring pad. Once the metal is clean, we sterilize with 90 percent alcohol or a 10-percent bleach solution. Then, carefully sharpen the tools for a safe and effective cut.

The following cuts are always mandatory and reflect the work of a pro.

All trees and woody shrubs have, if we look closely, usually two anatomical features: first, a branch collar or bulge at the base of a branch just as it grows out of a trunk or larger branch; and second, a branch, bark ridge, or furrow of bark pressed out of and between the trunk or main branch, and the smaller branch growing out from it. To promote proper healing, we always cut just outside — $\frac{1}{8}$ inch on a 1-inch diameter branch and $\frac{1}{4}$ inch on a larger branch — the branch bark ridge at an angle that mirrors the angle the branch bark ridge exhibits. We never ever cut off or within or violate the branch bark ridge because the cut cannot heal properly, which then encourages decay and leads to the decline and eventual death of the plant. The emphasis is placed on the proper branch bark ridge cut, but if we cannot see it — because of not looking closely enough for it — we always make an angled cut outside the branch collar. A cut that violates the branch bark ridge is called a flush cut and in basic terms reflects the work of an unskilled laborer.

On a branch with any weight on it — meaning about 3 feet long or longer and 3 to 4 inches in diameter or larger — we use a one, two, three cut. Cut number one would be out about a foot from the point of connection, cut from underneath, and at least a quarter of the way into the limb to up to about a third into it. A deeper cut may cause the weight of the limb to pinch and hold the blade, often making it impossible to remove it. Cut number two will be directly above cut number one to remove the limb. These two cuts are made to remove the limb a foot out and without tearing the bark, which is a severe injury to the tree. The third cut would be the final cut, about ¼ inch and angled, just outside the branch bark ridge. If you want to know the most important skills to prune properly, they are: clean, sharp tools, and the branch bark ridge. The rest is all window dressing.

The next important fundamental rule under health would be pruning for a healthy structure. Keep in mind that there are thousands of species of ornamental, not to mention fruiting, trees. There are varied shapes upright, like the Lombardy poplar; cone, like the pines; and round-headed, like most maples. The correct approach is to accentuate or complement the natural character of each plant. We should not attempt to force them into some sort of contrived form we imagine but accentuate their beauty instead.

With that in mind, we need to think of strength. We want to balance the foliage and, therefore, the weight distribution of the tree, helping to prevent future failures or broken branches. From a side view, we want to view the tree branches as balanced also. We want to plant in the young tree, and selectively remove branches in the established tree to balance the weight of the tree.

We do not want to look at the tree aesthetically or artistically, at least not at this point. We want to think of the branches as a skeleton developing. We want to encourage this symmetry, not in a controlled or contrived way but in a way to preserve the tree and complement its natural character.

— Chapter 3: —

Safety First

Although the word "pruning" does not conjure thoughts of a dangerous activity, pruning requires protection of the eyes, hands, legs, and feet because injuries can and do occur. For example, pruning tools, hedgers, and reciprocating saws can cut off fingers; falling tree limbs can cause head injuries; loud machinery can result in hearing loss; and flying debris and pieces of wood can cause eye injuries.

You should follow some basic safety rules when pruning. First and foremost, give your pruning job your undivided attention. Second, wear the proper protective gear, including safety goggles, gardening or pruning gloves, a hard hat, earplugs, and closed-toed shoes. Also, you should use the correct tools for the job, which depend on the pruning job and what it requires, and make sure that you use sharp tools. Finally, contact a professional if your pruning job involves trees near power lines, heavy limbs, or heights not safely reached by a ladder.

Eye and Ear Protection

The most common injury that results from pruning is eye injury so you should always wear eye protection, such as shatter-resistant safety glasses or goggles. A good rule of thumb is that if the growth to be removed is larger than what you can pinch off with a thumb and forefinger, then safety glasses are in order. A severe eye injury can occur quickly, especially if you feel fatigued, work in a hurry, or work in dim light. One misstep can send the end of a sharp-angled branch or a piece of flying wood deep into your eye tissue. After every major cut, you should step back and look at the tree or bush before making the next cut. This will allow you to reorient yourself to the size of the job, reconsider what limbs need pruning, and mentally note the location of the protruding limbs that can cause injury. Ear protection, such as earplugs, is also essential if working around chain saws. The Centers for Disease Control and Prevention reported that without proper hearing protection, running a chain saw for only two minutes can endanger your hearing. In addition, the U.S. Consumer Product Safety Commission stated that 36,000 people receive treatment in emergency rooms each year from chain saw accidents.

This man is wearing proper ear protection but needs protective goggles and gloves.

Hand Protection

Wearing a snug-fitting pair of leather work gloves is important to prevent injury to your hands from rough bark, thorns, and sharp blades. While you can purchase canvas gardening gloves, leather gloves can prevent sharp branches, thorns, and blades from penetrating through the glove. Find a nice pair of leather work gloves that feel comfortable and fit your hands properly. When working up close with multiple limbs and sharp blades, you can snip off a finger in an instant, even with the smaller pruning tool. A good pair of leather gloves can become a second skin, allowing you to feel the blade if it touches one hand before applying pressure to the cutting mechanism with the other. Avoid the type of clunky, leather work gloves that are too large and loose. You should reserve those kinds of gloves for working with shovels and rakes, not for pruning. They get in the way while you use most pruning tools and can lead to serious injury while working a chain saw because it is difficult to operate the small stop button or on-off switch, which is normally located in a tight place on the chain saw, when you have a bulky piece of leather in front of your finger. Although good leather gloves on average may cost more, they eventually shrink to custom fit your hand, and they can last for years. If you work outside often, buy two pairs and alternate between them to allow each pair to dry between uses. If you store your gloves in a barn or shed, always shake them out before you put them on. Scorpions and brown recluse spiders love to hide in dark, damp places.

You should invest in a good pair of leather gloves to reduce the risk of injury.

Foot and Leg Protection

Most tools with blades attached will land with the sharp end pointing down because the sharp end tends to be heavier. One exception to this rule is a chain saw, which has the heavy engine housing on the other end that can smash your feet instead. This is why it is dangerous to work with pruning tools when you wear light shoes, such gardening clogs or tennis shoes. Leather boots that have ankle support are the best shoe choice when pruning because a dropped tool cannot pierce them, and they can also prevent a twisted ankle if you walk or work on uneven ground. If you work in rural areas where snakes live, leather boots can afford you some protection in case you step on one while you are concentrating on the task at hand. Another reason for heavy boots is that long thorns easily puncture the soles of light shoes, as anyone who has ever stepped on a branch from a lemon or wild apple tree can tell you. For heavier jobs, such as working with heavy branches or larger trees, and when working in heavy brush, wearing a pair of leather chaps or leggings is also appropriate. Made of leather or thick cotton, they provide protection from an accident if you use a chain saw or a large blade, such as a machete or shearing knife, which people use to trim evergreens. A nifty trick used by professionals who use a shearing knife is to hold something in your empty hand, such as a rock, so you never are handling a branch with that hand when you bring the blade down to cut a branch, thus preventing the possibility of cutting off one of your own limbs.

Working Around Electricity

Never take for granted that a utility line is not working or is far enough away from a nearby limb to prevent electrocution. When a tree touches a utility line, the electricity can be redirected into the tissue of the tree. This means that electrocution can occur if anyone or anything touches the tree or stands on the ground within several feet of the tree. If you are pruning a tree and a limb or a pruning tool touches a power line, you could sustain injuries or die. Trees growing close to a power line create an unusual situation because electricity from the power line can arc or jump from the power line to a nearby tree. If a tree is located near a power line, it is always best to consult or hire a professional to remove that limb.

You do not just need to worry about electricity from power lines when pruning. There are different pruning tools available on the market powered by electricity. While these tools are not as noisy or as high maintenance as gas-powered tools, they are not less dangerous. While the blades alone can cause severe injury, keep in mind that you are also working around electricity. Although the cord attached to an electric hedge trimmer is normally ridiculously short, you inevitably attach that short cord to a 100-foot extension cord. That much cord around you while you work can create a tripping hazard. While difficult when you are trying to work, you must avoid cutting into the line with the trimmer. If you do, dispose of the extension cord and buy another. Never attempt to patch the cord: The tape will eventually pull off or wear away, leaving an exposed area that can electrocute someone if they step on it. Also, damp ground around the bare area of the cord can become energized and cause electrocution. You can purchase a new, outdoor extension cord at the discount store for fewer than $10 so it is better to buy a new one for your safety rather than risk patching one with tape. If the electric hedge trimmer or chain saw clogs or needs maintenance, unplug it before taking it apart or poking it with a metal tool. Never use an electric-powered trimmer or saw to cut overhead limbs because the cord can become tangled in the branches when they fall, causing you to lose control of the trimmer. Before starting any pruning job, you need to read and re-read all safety precautions that come with any power tool.

Securing the Area

Anytime you use power tools, you must secure the area by removing anything that obstructs your ability to move freely. If you will cut large limbs with a chain saw, you must clear the area around a tree where limbs may fall of pets, children, and vehicles. Be aware of other plants that might get damaged from falling limbs. For smaller jobs, clear the immediate area around the bushes or plants of items that are not permanent fixtures in that area. Removing the items gives you a sense of perspective while working and prevents you from making a cut that creates an uneven or out-of-balance appearance. If you prune around an item instead of moving that item, the bush will look uneven once you remove the item. Never operate power tools or handle items with sharp blades after drinking alcohol or taking drugs that impair your judgment. It only takes one second to make a bad decision that can affect you for a lifetime.

Chapter 4:

The Right Tool for the Job

You must choose the correct pruning tool because it affects the well-being of the tree or shrub, and it can also protect your safety. Choosing the wrong tool can affect the outcome of your pruning job, not to mention leave you frustrated. Try not to get overwhelmed when shopping for your tools, although the variety of tools can overwhelm a beginner. Some pruning tools are job-specific, while others are universal. The bottom line is you do not need a large or expensive variety of pruning tools to do the right job. You will only need a few basic tools to handle home pruning jobs. And if you happen to be left-handed, tools exist for southpaws, too.

You can purchase gardening tools at hardware stores, as well as in the gardening section of large department stores.

Choosing the Right Tool

When you have decided on which tool to use for pruning, remember the tool is specific to the job. For instance, using a chain saw to cut small branches on a plum tree results in excessive damage to the tissue of the plum tree, but at the same time, using a small hand-held pruning tool to cut a large limb can break the tool or result in an untidy or incomplete cut. Saws made for pruning have wider and longer teeth than a wood saw a carpenter might use. The saw's teeth are designed so they do not get clogged with green plant tissue during the cutting process. If you ever try to cut a green tree limb with a carpenter's saw, it quickly becomes apparent the saw will not work. After two or three thrusts, you can no longer use the saw.

For your safety and to keep your tools like new, be sure to use proper equipment appropriate for pruning.

Shears

Four types of gardening tools are considered shears: anvil shears; bypass shears, also known as hand shears; manual shears; and electric shears. You use **shears** for lighter work, such as creating a hedge or for cutting limbs up to ½ inch in diameter. They cost less than most pruning tools, but the low cost means they do not work well and break quickly. The best quality shears have removable blades you can sharpen and parts you can easily replace if they wear out.

1. Anvil Shears

Anvil shears have one blade instead of two. When you squeeze the handle, you push the main or top blade down into a flat section of soft metal called the anvil. Anvil shears are cheap — less than $10 — and because of the low quality, anvil shears have a tendency to break. They create a poor cut because no follow through from a second or bottom blade occurs. Once the top blade becomes dull, the anvil and dull blade simply crush the plant tissue, causing it to separate when you squeeze the handle. You should only use an anvil shear for the lightest work, such as clipping houseplants, thin-stemmed flowers, or small twigs.

2. Bypass Shears

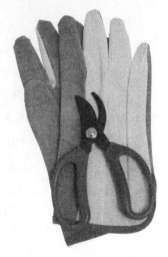

A bypass shear may cost a little more but can offer a valuable addition to your pruning equipment. It could soon become your most used tool in the garden. Many of the better models have a tension screw to keep them closed. You can carry a bypass shear in a pocket as long as it has a safety catch to lock it closed, or you can place it in a holder worn on your belt. You can completely take apart a good bypass shear for blade sharpening, cleaning, and oiling. A bypass shear has two blades and works like a pair of scissors, where one blade is closely aligned with another, and they slide past each other, making a clean cut. Use bypass shears for pruning branches and stems up to ½ inch in diameter.

3. Manual Shears

Most people think of manual shears when they hear the word shears. Manual shears are long and pointed and are made in the bypass style of two blades that work like scissors. You use them for cutting large amounts of leaves and small branches at one time. People most often use manual shears for creating a long hedge by trimming all the bushes in a row to the same height and width. They also use manual shears to shape solitary plants into specific or whimsical shapes. Manual shears are a challenge to use because you must have an eye for the shape you are trying to create while manually chopping the leaves and branches for a long time. They can also tire you out quicker than electric shears because they require more physical energy on your part.

4. Electric Shears

Electric shears are the modern cousin of the manual shears. The blades slide forward and backward against a stationary row of metal teeth. As the electric shear passes over the small branches and leaves of the shrubbery, the branches slip into the gaps between the stationary teeth, and the sliding blades snip them off. An electric shear is an invaluable tool for a big shearing job that might involve hours of tedious work using a manual shear because less exertion is used; the electrical automatic sliding of the blades means a quicker cut with less effort exuded. Electric shears are one of the most popular pruning tools because they are fast, easy to handle, precise, and less tiring.

Loppers

You use loppers for cutting limbs from ½ to 2 inches in diameter, depending on the model. Loppers are also good for reaching into overgrown brush and brambles to make a pruning cut. The cutting mechanism of a lopper is similar to the hand shears, meaning there are anvil and bypass types. The handles of a lopper are much longer than a hand shear and provide leverage when applying pressure for cutting large branches.

If cutting dead or dry wood, an anvil-style lopper works better, and for live wood, the bypass lopper works better. Dry wood has the tendency to get stuck between the blades of a bypass lopper and can cause the tool to bend or break as immense pressure is applied to the blade when the long handles are squeezed together. Some people prefer wooden handles because they absorb shock and are more comfortable for your hands, but wooden handles make the tool heavier, which can tire you out quickly. Some of the newer models are made with strong, lightweight metals and are great for big jobs where you might carry the tool all day. Once again, a more expensive model you can take apart, oil, clean, and sharpen is your best choice.

Pole pruner

A pole pruner is lightweight pole made of plastic or fiberglass that may have a saw blade, a bypass tool, or both mechanisms attached to one end. The pole is usually 4 to 6 feet long, with some models providing even longer poles. The bypass tool attached to a pole pruner works like a bypass shear except one blade remains stationary and the other blade has a long rope or cord attached to it in the area where the handle would normally be. When you pull the cord, it cuts the branch as the blades close together. A spring is fastened between the blade handles so the blade snaps open after the cut is completed and the cord is released. For larger limbs, the saw portion is placed against the limb and the pole is manually moved up and down until the limb is cut and falls away.

A pole pruner looks safe enough, but it is actually one of the more dangerous pruning tools because you are working almost directly underneath the limbs you are removing, and they can fall on you. Although that may sound dangerous, it is not even the most dangerous part of working with a pole trimmer. The most dangerous part is the blade can loosen while you saw the limb and fall into your face while you look up to see what you are doing. For that reason, when using a pole trimmer, position yourself so that the branches and mechanical parts cannot fall on you. Better yet, if you require a pole pruner because limbs are out of reach, you should hire a professional arborist to do the job. Also, always avoid using an aluminum pole pruner around power lines, or you risk electrocution.

Saws

Pruning saws are used when your pruning job involves heavy work involving thicker limbs, such as when you need to cut a branch that is more than ¾ inch in diameter. Shears do not work well on thicker wood because shears tend to either break or squeeze the limb being cut and damage its bark. When cutting live branches, you should use a pruning saw and not a carpenter's saw, as previously mentioned. Carpenter's saws work effectively on dead wood only because they get sticky and clogged when cutting live branches.

1. D-shaped and pointed-nose bow saws

As mentioned before, a wood saw has bigger teeth with wider spaces between them than a carpenter's saw so plant tissue does not collect in the teeth while working. A D-shaped bow saw looks like a D and has a metal frame that curves over the straight blade. The metal frame provides strength so the blade cannot twist or crumple when you apply pressure as you push or pull the saw. You should not confuse it with a traditional woodworking tool, also called a bow saw, which has a small blade and a wooden frame. A D-shaped bow saw comes as small as 21 inches long or big enough for two people to use, with each person commandeering one end of the saw.

Another similar tool is the pointed-nose bow saw, which is similar to the D-shaped bow saw but the end opposite the handle end is tapered or narrowed. This tool works great in tight or overgrown areas. For example, a pointed bow saw comes in handy when cutting the lower limbs from a tree, such as a cedar, that may have hundreds of limbs interfering with the cutting process.

2. Curved-blade saws

Curved-blade saws are also known as pull saws because the cutting action occurs when you pull the saw toward you. You operate a curved-blade saw with one hand, and most models have blades around 12 inches in length with a 5- or 6-inch handle. You can fold and carry some types in a pocket, while you hold others in a saw holder. They are handy for the professional gardener or landscaper because they are lightweight and can remove limbs up to 1½ inches in diameter.

Curved-blade saw. Image courtesy of the USDA.

3. Electric- and gasoline-powered chain saws

A chain saw is considered one of the most dangerous hand tools you can purchase, with more than 36,000 injuries and deaths reported each year in the United States alone. Chain saws come in all sizes, from lightweight models with 10-inch chains and holding bars used for simple landscape maintenance to 42-inch monsters used for felling large trees. To determine the right saw for your job, buy a chain saw with a bar length half the size of your largest project. For example, if the largest tree or branch you plan to ever cut is 20 inches in diameter, you need a 10-inch saw blade, which is 10 inches for each side of the branch or tree. Gas chain saws must have the right mixture of oil and gasoline in the fuel tank per the saw's manual and should be kept clean and oiled to prevent rust. Drain the fuel and oil the chain and bar if you will keep the chain saw in storage for any length of time, such as over the winter.

Electric chain saws rarely have longer than a 12-inch bar and are designed for pruning work and cutting down trees and shrubs with smaller diameters. The electric cord can become a

Chain saw. Image courtesy of the USDA.

hazard when working in thick brush or close quarters, but electric chain saws start up when you are ready to go to work. The same cannot be said for a gas-powered chain saw, no matter how well-maintained you keep it.

All chain saws have blades that dull quickly, and you must sharpen them often. A chain saw should cut through wood quickly and effortlessly. A dull blade makes the saw and the operator work harder than needed. A dull saw can be dangerous because it cuts slowly and will catch on the wood you are cutting, causing you to easily lose control of the saw and harm yourself. You can always buy a new blade when one dulls, but it is inconvenient and expensive to run to the hardware store to replace a perfectly good blade every time you need to do a job. You can buy an inexpensive chain saw blade sharpener or file the shape of a number two pencil but a little thinner. To sharpen the blade, simply run the sharpener back and forth between the teeth of the chain saw blade. Although this may take some time to get used to, sharpening a blade is cheaper than buying a new one. If sharpening a chain saw blade makes you nervous, you may want to leave sharpening the blade to an expert.

4. Reciprocating saw

A reciprocating, or oscillating, saw is a small electrical or battery-powered saw used for a variety of household chores. Carpenters and sheet rock workers commonly use this tool. It is called a reciprocating saw because the blade moves back and forth so one motion "reciprocates" for the other motion. You can use this saw as a pruning tool as long as you remember to install a blade into the saw that is specific to pruning before you begin your pruning job. This pruning blade has large, aggressive teeth and comes in 9-inch and 12-inch sizes. If you prune with a woodworking blade installed, you run the risk of the blade jamming halfway through the project or breaking the blade. You can use reciprocating saws for pruning large branches, as well as cutting down small trees and shrubs.

Ladders

A ladder is an important tool often used by the pruning professional and homeowner. A step ladder that opens into a small A-frame suits most small jobs where you need to extend your reach a few feet. When it comes to accessing higher limbs, you should choose an extension ladder that telescopes upward. It allows you to put the top of the ladder a foot or so above or so above the limb you intend to prune or against or against the tree trunk; you can also tie it to the tree for extra stability. Pruning involves a constant shift in weight, as well as some physical exertion that can destabilize an A-frame ladder on soft or uneven ground so you want to make sure your ladder is stable. Also, consider purchasing a ladder made with lightweight materials, such as aluminum and fiberglass because this material can last for many years. Wooden ladders decay from exposure to the elements and are heavy to move around the garden, but a wooden ladder offers a safer choice if pruning near electrical wires because aluminum ladders can be conduits for electricity.

Tool Maintenance and Storage

Good pruning tools are expensive but can last for years, if properly maintained. You should change bow saw blades when they become dull, and you can sharpen shear and lopper blades by taking the tool apart and placing the blades one at a time in a vice grip with the blade up and the handle toward you.

Then, take an ordinary 10-inch mill file, and drag it across the blade in an upward motion to sharpen the blades. A mill file, also known as a diamond file, can have a single or dual row of teeth. You

These vintage pitted pruning shears are still in good condition because of proper maintenance.

should use a 10-inch mill file because it is the correct coarseness for sharpening shears, and an 8-inch mill file is too fine. Keep in mind that you want to improve the edge already placed there by the factory, which calibrated it to be in the right position for when it meets the other blade. If you get carried away and file it until the blade is angled in another direction, the tool cannot cut properly when you put the tool back together, no matter how sharp you make it. A rule of thumb is to sharpen your tools once every six weeks — or once a year if you do not prune often. If you maintain your pruning tools and sharpen them often, then it should only take about ten minutes to run your blades against the file. Ten to 20 draws with a mill file should do the trick, but if you do not keep your tools sharp and you allow them to get dull, then you may need to do 40 to 50 passes.

Before storing all tools, wipe the metal blades with an oily rag, lightly oil the moving parts, and hang them up, if possible, on nails or pegs on a wall in your shed or garage. You might want to use a pegboard or plywood sheet. This keeps them handy, all in one place, and prevents rust on the metal surfaces. Plus, you can easily

It is helpful to have a gardener's bag to carry with you as you prune your trees.

identify which tools you may be missing or may have left outside. To preserve your tools, rub any wooden handles with a rag that contains a little linseed oil. It is especially important to properly store your tools before winter so that when spring arrives, they are in good shape and ready to go.

Chapter 5:

General Pruning Rules

Once you have the correct tools in place to handle the job you want to tackle, you will want to make sure you do your pruning at the correct time of year, depending on the tree or shrub you will prune. You should prune in late winter, between late February or early March, just before the leaf and flower buds begin to swell. This allows the plant to heal faster than if pruned in late summer or fall when the plant has less moisture available to seal off wounds and growth slows down. Of course, late winter can mean different times, depending on where you live, but it occurs when the days begin to get longer and warm up, but no sign of swelling buds or new growth exists.

Exceptions to every rule exist. For example, plants that bloom in the spring, such as azaleas or gardenias, require pruning right after blooming because they prepare to bloom the following spring in mid-summer and fall. Because of the tremendous differences in weather conditions throughout

This person is pruning a tree in March before it has its new buds.

North America, there are no hard and fast rules of when to prune and when not to prune. As in the case of spring bloomers, as mentioned before, it really does depend on where you live and what plant you prune. Many gardeners prefer late winter pruning because most trees and shrubs are dormant and less likely to bleed excessive amounts of sap. Plants pruned in late winter include fruit trees, roses, broad-leaf evergreens, vines, and some flowering trees. Spring is good for prune repair of trees and shrubs damaged by ice, snow, or wind or those with wounds caused by animals or winter sportsmen. Spring is also a good time to pinch off buds that are starting branches in the wrong places, as well as suckers, water sprouts, or branches growing in the wrong direction.

Summer, when plants tend to do the most growing, is a good time to shear evergreens and hedges and also to prune shrubs that bloom in spring, such as the above mentioned azaleas and gardenias, as well as lilac, bridal wreath, honeysuckle, and spires. Late summer is also a favorable time to prune certain trees, such as birches and maples because these trees tend to bleed heavily when pruned in winter. If you live in the north, fall is a good time to cut back roses, clematis, hydrangea, crape myrtle, hibiscus, and other shrubs. You should know the correct time to prune according to your location. This book attempts to give a general idea of when to prune individual types of trees and shrubs, but you should confirm the proper time to prune for your specific climate. Pruning at the wrong time could cost you your plant.

Cutting at the Bud

A **bud** is an undeveloped leaf or potential branch. In cooler climates, tiny buds form during the winter just under the bark layer and emerge in late winter covered with scales that protect the tender buds from the freezing weather. In warmer climates, many plants have no protective scales, and the unprotected bud grows rapidly as soon as the days get long enough to justify a break in dormancy; these are known as **naked buds**. Once the buds begin to emerge, they are named according to where they appear on the branch. The buds at the tip end of the branch are called **terminal buds,** and those on the sides of the branches are called **lateral buds**.

The correct place to cut the branch is at an angle — the top should be a ¼ inch above a desirable lateral bud. A **desirable bud** is a lateral bud that will grow from the side of a branch when it emerges. For example, if a tree has a lateral bud on the outside of the limb and you cut the branch above that bud, it will grow in an outward direction. Cutting the stem at an angle above the lateral bud allows water to run off the new cut so it receives adequate hydration. If you cut too close to the new bud, the bud may die, and if you cut too far away, the branch will die back to the bud area and possibly kill the bud so keep in mind the ¼-inch distance when cutting small branches — those about a ¼ inch in diameter — with anvil or bypass shears. For larger branches that require a lopper pruner because of their height or thicker diameter, the same rules apply, although the branch you cut may not have buds but small branches going in every direction. An easy rule of thumb is you always cut a large branch back to a live branch that is growing in the desired direction or to the main trunk of the tree. Do not leave a stub because this could rot and leave the tree open to disease or insect infestation.

If you will cut branches in order to provide access to the area underneath a tree canopy, you may only need to cut the main limbs back to an upward growing stem with a lopper rather than cutting lower limbs with a saw. If you cut only a portion of a diseased or dead limb and you do not want to remove the entire limb, cut the limb back at least 6 inches beyond the damaged area to a branch or bud growing in the desired direction. It may seem effective to cut back the branch just past the diseased part because of the branch, but you should remove the entire diseased branch back to a main stem. Removing the entire branch will ensure you have totally removed the disease. Also, make sure you do not leave the diseased or insect-ridden branch on the ground because diseased spores and insects can make their way back to the tree or into the soil and re-infect your plant. Instead, compost, burn, or destroy the removed branch, and remember to clean your pruning tools with alcohol or a 10-percent bleach solution so that you do not infect other plants in your yard.

Buds are classified as either alternating, opposite, or whorled. **Whorled buds**, such as those found on most evergreens, occur when three or more buds position themselves around the stem, in the same location at the stem. The above example of pruning in relation to leaf buds considers alternating buds only, which form on alternating positions along the branches. By cutting above an **alternating bud** growing in a desirable direction, you can encourage growth in that direction. On some bushy plants and some trees, such as maple and dogwood, you will find buds and leaf growth located directly across the stem from each other. These are called **opposite buds**, and the thickened area from where they grow is called the **leaf node**. In this case, the growth habit is different and cannot be controlled in a way that forces growth into one direction unless you take an extra step when pruning; that is, you cut at an angle a ¼ inch above the leaf node with the high end of the angle above the bud you will leave on the plant. Then pull or twist off the other bud.

People prune shrubs with opposite buds to encourage thicker growth or to shorten an unruly plant. If you do not remove one bud at the pruning cut, growth will resume at the same rate from both buds, creating thicker growth. If you prune in an area too high on bushes with opposite buds, the plant can become top heavy and prone to sprawling or breaking in high winds. You should only prune a tree that

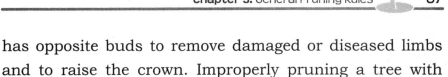

has opposite buds to remove damaged or diseased limbs and to raise the crown. Improperly pruning a tree with opposite buds creates uneven and excessive tender growth susceptible to freeze and insect damage.

Think of the worst pruning job you have ever seen; it was most likely done on a tree with opposite buds that was whacked off at one level, an action known as **topping**. Hundreds of small branches grew in to replace the removed limbs and created that weedy and unnatural look to the landscape. You can only make a tree with an opposite budding structure look good after topping by cutting out or thinning the new growth, which further weakens the tree, leaving it susceptible to insect damage and disease. If a tree with opposite buds needs severe pruning, such as when one grows into a power line, you should have the tree completely removed by a professional arborist, rather than trying to solve the problem with a drastic pruning program like topping. A professional will have experience in working around power lines and will know how to save the tree since topping will only cause the tree to weaken and become susceptible to insect damage and disease. If the crown of a tree has alternative buds that need reducing, a creative and experienced arborist may save the tree. Although subsequent growth will not be as weak as the growth from a tree that produces opposite buds, the tree will require several professional pruning sessions to keep it healthy and attractive.

Four Ways to Prune Trees and Shrubs

By now, you should know the main reasons for pruning a tree or shrub and the right tools to accomplish the job. Now, it is time to take a look at general pruning rules because you should prune a tree or bush in a certain way. Whether you will prune large trees, small trees, or shrubs, there are four different places to make a cut:

1. Where the target branch meets a main branch of the trunk of the tree.
2. At the ground level.
3. Above a bud.
4. Above a healthy side branch.

As you know, improper pruning methods can adversely affect both the short- and long-term health of a tree or shrub, not to mention they can also make your plant look unattractive. Trees sustain damage during the pruning process when a heavy branch is cut improperly. When you are use loppers with sharp and well-maintained blades, you should be able to obtain a clean cut as you cut the limb away from the tree just outside the branch collar. The collar allows a limb to eventually break away cleanly from the main trunk or limb without damaging the main stem or trunk. In nature, this natural pruning process does not always occur as it is supposed to because dead or damaged branches can fall off and leave a jagged wound that is susceptible to disease or insect infestation. A sizeable wound leaves the tree with an unsightly appearance and can lead to the death of the tree. That is why pruning is looked at as a way to complement the natural shape or habit of a tree or shrub and a way to ward off the inevitable and extend the natural life of the tree or shrub.

In nature, a damaged or diseased limb dies and decays all the way back to the collar in a process that may take several years. Once the limb breaks away from the collar or completely decays, the tree detects that the branch is no longer a part of the structure, and cellular activity within the collar ceases. Then, the cells located outside the collar begin the process of sealing the wound from any encroaching decay or disease by producing woody growth that eventually closes over the wound. Because the tree cannot begin the process of closing over the area where the dead limb was located until the branch is gone, it creates a special problem.

Letting nature take its course is not always the best solution because when a large limb dies, it may take many years for the limb to finally fall away from the tree. As the large limb slowly decays, the area inside the branch collar becomes dormant, and over time, it also begins to decay. As the years pass, a cavity forms in the trunk of the tree inside the collar from where the large limb grew. When the large limb falls away, the gaping hole becomes visible. By now, the decay from the dormant area inside the root collar may have reached deep into the heartwood, the part of the tree that gives it strength and resistance from high winds and ice storms. Although animals use large holes or cavities in trees as shelter and they are interesting to see, they are potentially fatal to the tree. Constant moisture running into the hole continues to rot the heartwood, weakening it until the trunk snaps in high wind or the tree simply falls apart, rotting from the inside out. You can repair cavities already formed in the side of an older tree by scraping out the rotted wood and then filling the wound with tree cavity filler. Once you fill the cavity with tree cavity filler, the naturally occurring healing process begins as the collar expands and closes over the wound. The best approach is to never let cavities form by properly cutting away dead or diseased branches at the branch collar as needed. This is why pruning a tree is the better solution than letting a tree naturally decay.

The three-step cutting method

Most people think cutting a limb by sawing away at the top of the branch surface will eventually make the limb fall magically away from the tree. The good news is the limb will eventually fall, but the bad news is the bottom of the limb still attached to the tree will most likely pull a strip of bark and tree tissue down with it, leaving the tree with an exposed wound.

The proper way to cut a big limb and prevent damage to the tree is to cut the limb in three stages.

1. Start by making an undercut 6 inches from the branch collar. This should be at least one-quarter of the way through the branch. If you are using a chain saw, you will pull the top

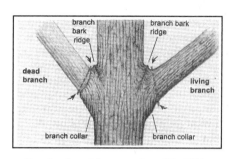

Targeting the cut. Image courtesy of the USDA.

of the blade into the bottom of the branch to create the cut.

2. Then, begin the cut from the top about 1 inch beyond the bottom cut. This cut is on the side of the bottom cut that is away from the tree. Cut completely

Left image: Cutting a smaller branch. Right image: Cutting a larger branch. Image courtesy of the USDA.

through the limb and the limb will come off cleanly as it falls away, leaving a 6-inch stub.

3. The final cut is made at the collar to remove the remaining stub. If the branch is large and you are afraid of it crashing down and damaging something,

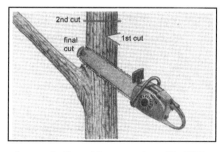

Crown reduction cut. Image courtesy of the USDA.

tie one end of a long rope around the limb you will cut, and throw the other end of the rope over a sturdy higher limb. Then, tie the other end of the rope to a stable object on the ground. After you cut the big limb, untie the rope from the stable object, and using the higher limb as a pulley, hold on to the free end of the rope, and slowly lower the heavy limb to the ground.

What about pruning paints?

Gardeners and arborists debate about whether to use **pruning paints** or sealants, which are applied on the freshly cut area to protect the tree from insects attracted to the sap that could spread diseases. Some experts claim that a tree heals better without the use of pruning paint on new cuts and wounds, while others believe sealants and pruning paints prevent the tree from bleeding excessively. Both sides of the issue are partially correct. In warmer climates, where diseases such as **oak wilt** — a disease caused by a fungus that causes oak trees to drop their leaves and wilt — are ravaging landscapes, pruning paint is highly recommended because the beetle that spreads oak wilt is attracted to fresh sap. People can also apply pruning paint where extensive mechanical damage occurs around the bottom of the tree from landscaping equipment. Trees like evergreens, such as pines and arborvitae, have no need for pruning paints because they supply sap quickly to the damaged area, which seals any wounds. Those in favor of using pruning paint feel it should be applied to all cuts on older trees and all cuts on valuable hardwoods — no matter the age — to prevent rot or insect infestation. Those opposed to the use of pruning paint argue that it contains chemicals that can prevent the tree from naturally sealing its wounds and can also crack, allowing water to collect behind the paint, leading to rot. When deciding whether to use a sealant or pruning paint, you should know that these paints could actually act as a cover for insects, who can then nest in the wound. Although some trees will get wounded from situations you cannot control, prune in the right time of year to keep from further harming your tree.

Know when not to prune

When a deciduous shade tree is a young tree, it produces many side branches. While these side branches give the tree an unsightly and unkempt look, they are an important part of the growing process. A young tree has small roots attached to the trunk of the tree just under the soil line. These young roots are an important part of the root structure. When the wind violently whips the young tree around during a storm, the small roots can break away from the trunk. When this happens, it affects the health and vigor of the young tree because roots are a tree's pipeline to nutrients and water, as well as its means of gripping the soil so that it is not damaged and blown over in windy conditions. Young trees can adapt to having small roots by growing numerous side branches to catch the wind instead of allowing themselves to be whipped around. A young tree pruned into a cotton swab shape — with all the growth on top — is susceptible to wind damage and must be staked or protected with a tree guard, which is a type of fence that has its shape and height dependent upon the type of tree or bush you will protect.

The best approach is to allow the tree to grow into its natural shape until it is a few years old and stands 12 to 16 feet tall because, as previously stated, a young tree has a small root system so it needs its lower branches on its sides to catch the wind while maintaining minimal damage. As your tree grows, cut the branches from the bottom up a few times each year until the amount of clearance from the ground is desired. This method is called **crown lifting**, or basal pruning, and results in a stronger tree with a heavier trunk and stronger root system. For best results, only crown lift an amount of limbs at one time that equals a space one-fifth of the height of the tree. For example, if a young tree is 15 feet tall, only cut enough limbs to equal a space that is 3 feet from the ground. Once you have cut all the branches to a space one-fifth of the height of the tree, wait two or three years before cutting more limbs from the bottom using the same ratio. If you plant a tree in the proper place according to the eventual size of the tree, then you will not need to perform any pruning outside of basal pruning except to remove dead limbs. It is important to do this early shaping because it is easier to cut off the bottom branches while these limbs are still small. In addition, smaller pruned branches leave smaller wounds. If you do not do this basal pruning while the tree is young — that is, younger than 5 years old — and you find that your tree has large limbs growing too low to the ground, make sure your tree has a good top growth before you prune any bottom branches. *For more information about crown lifting, see Chapter 7.*

What About Bushes?

People prune bushes to create fuller and healthier-looking plants; to give the bush only a few main limbs in order to highlight unusual or interesting stem growth; or to encourage larger blooms. Deciduous flowering shrubs rarely need pruning outside of removing dead wood or thinning out wood growing too thickly, but certain perennial shrubs, such as butterfly bushes and crape myrtles, which die to the ground every winter, must have all of the old growth removed before spring. But, certain shrubs, such as the four-wing saltbush and mountain mahogany, are semi-evergreen, and you should not remove old stem growth until spring when you can easily find the dead growth. Once you prune the dead growth, you can attractively shape the live growth as needed. Cutting a semi-evergreen shrub completely to the ground every winter can set it back or even shock it to the point of decline or death. Although it is recommended that you prune young trees and bushes in the winter, severe pruning of plants with green stems or thin bark layers can make the plant more vulnerable to cold weather. For example, when a citrus tree that usually has a thin layer of bark because of its adaptation to warmer climates grows in a marginal area — an area that has mild winters but is not as cold as the winters in northern regions — without protection, it could possibly freeze during the winter. It grows quite large and healthy, albeit unruly, over the years. The owner then decides to prune the citrus tree back into a nice tree form in the coldest part of winter, and the 10-year-old citrus tree suddenly dies. Shock resulting from the drastic pruning followed by another cold snap caused the decline of the tree.

Although most shrubs rarely need pruning, except to remove dead wood or to thin a thick bush, you need to remove all suckers from the base of the bush. You also might want to prune older, taller branches to keep your bush looking neater. Prune off any dead or damaged branches on the top and any branches that cross each other or appear weak and thin. Cut back the tips of straggly growths. As your bush grows, prune only when necessary to shape it.

If you want to create a thicker, bushier shrub, cut back new shoots about halfway. Before cutting, check to see if your bush's branches have alternate leaves. If it does, cut to an outward-facing bud so you do not create crowded branches growing in the center of the plant. If your bush has opposite leaves on its branches, cut where you want new branches to grow. Also, removing fading flowers on flowering shrubs helps promote more flower growth the following year. If you have a spring-blooming shrub that blooms on wood grown in the previous year, prune and thin after it blooms. If you have a summer- or fall-blooming shrub that blooms on new wood, prune in early spring.

You can perform most pruning done on shrubs with pruning shears. If you need to reach into the center of the bush, use long loppers. If your bush is a hedge, prune with hedge shears, although you can trim stray growths with pruning shears.

Other Pruning Rules

Be aware of the natural shape of a bush or tree. There is no point in destroying what took Mother Nature years to develop, unless you are creating an artistic shape with a technique like pleaching. *For more information about pleaching, see Chapter 7.* You can make your job as a pruner or landscaper easier by simply enhancing what already occurs in nature rather than trying to replace it. Trying to replace what is already a perfect system takes constant vigilance. You can do it, as when you change the natural shape of a tree or bush, but remember: The tree or bush will always attempt to grow back to its natural shape. Therefore, the amount of pruning you will have to do will depend on whether you choose to let a plant grow in its natural shape or in a shape you have created. Some pruning methods, although interesting and capable of beautiful results, require ongoing maintenance and a large investment in time and energy because the plant will soon grow and return to its natural shape.

If you are choosing plants for your landscape, choose plants suitable for the space and plants that need little pruning and maintenance, such as most shrubs and trees allowed to grow in their natural shape like most deciduous shade trees. The extra work involved in an ongoing pruning program may be easy and fun when you are young, but it will get tiresome as you get older. For example, a new homeowner buys a Chinese wisteria vine and trains it into a beautiful bush form. A Chinese wisteria vine can be beautiful with its purple flower but is also considered an invasive plant. Every year, the homeowner carefully clips away old growth so it stays compact and attractive. The drooping fragrant clusters of purple flowers that appear in spring are the envy of the neighborhood. Then the homeowner gets a promotion at work and has less spare time to devote to gardening. Within three years, that same wisteria vine that was the envy of the neighbors is now their worst enemy because it rambles uncontrolled over their trees and homes. It would have been a better idea if the new homeowner had thought long-term and purchased a flowering shrub that would provide the same results without the eventual headaches. You need to consider the amount of dedication your plants will require, both now and in the future.

If the tree or shrub you are thinking about pruning is not creating an immediate problem in the landscape, take your time deciding where and how to prune. It may take a year or more of carefully studying your subject to get the best results. While it is obvious that you need to prune dead or diseased branches, keep in mind that it is better to take a pruning job slowly, rather than prune too much too quickly and then not be satisfied with the results, or worse, put the tree in a state of shock from which it cannot recover. Before deciding how to prune your plants consider these variables:

- **Sunlight:** You should take note of what angle the sun shines on your subject during different times of the year. You may find that if you basal prune a shade tree located on the south side of a house, the winter sun that remains low on the horizon can shine under the tree canopy and warm the house. During the summer, when the sun is high in the sky, that same tree can shade the house during the hottest part of the day.

- **Location:** If you are new to an area and have many different trees or shrubs in the landscape you are unfamiliar with, wait a year to see what blooms in the spring and what produces a multitude of beautiful fall colors. The idea of waiting a year to prune a new landscape is especially important if you are a new resident in a rural area where unfamiliar plants are everywhere. Finding out that you have destroyed an established grove of valuable dogwoods that were blocking your view is a feeling no one should have to experience.

- **Shape:** It is also important to understand the natural shape of a tree before you lop off unnecessary branches. Always prune off dead branches or branches that cross because these can affect the health of the tree.

Although most of the pruning rules require restraint and careful planning, one situation where pruning is always necessary for the health and vigor of a tree or bush exists: the removal of suckers and water sprouts. **Water sprouts** are vigorous green limbs, mostly seen on fruit trees and rose bushes, which emerge from an existing mature branch. You can easily see them because their fast-growing green shoots look different than the rest of the plant. They rarely produce fruit or flowers and draw energy from the rest of the plant. Remove water sprouts by cutting at the collar where they meet a main branch. Water sprouts also commonly appear right below the root graft. The **root graft** is the thickened offset area at the base of a single trunk tree or bush where a type of root system with certain favorable characteristics is grafted to a plant with other desirable characteristics. Root grafting is a natural occurrence that takes place under the soil, where as roots grow, they cross each other and eventually fuse or grow together. For example, the root system of a wild fruit tree resistant to nematodes may be grafted to a fruit tree resistant to certain fungal diseases. If you allow the water sprouts that appear below the root graft to grow, the area above the root graft that produces the high-quality fruit will die as the vigorous water sprouts take all the energy away from top growth. This means any fruit that normally would grow below the root graft would die or not grow. Use a pair of sharp pruning shears to cut the water sprouts back to the base of the tree. Also, ripping water sprouts off with a quick jerk of your hand will reduce new sprouts from growing from the same point. Simply cutting the sprouts and not removing the entire plant will not stop the sprouts from growing back.

Suckers — also called root suckers, which are also a form of water sprouts — come up from the underground roots of trees and are a natural part of the reproduction process of many trees and shrubs. If allowed to grow, they can come up by the hundreds, interfering with lawn equipment and becoming unsightly to your groomed landscape. They can also produce useless fruit and can weaken the tree. As mentioned in the section about water sprouts, you can cut suckers, but you are better off eliminating them by simply jerking them out with your hand. This will prevent them from regrowing. Never use an herbicide on suckers because they are a part of the tree or shrub, and the herbicide can possibly kill the main plant. If the suckers grow from a plant growing on its own root system and is not root grafted, you can start a new plant identical to the main plant by cutting away a sucker. Leave some roots on the sucker intact and replant it in another location or in a container, but do not remove suckers during the spring because this could cause the tree to excessively bleed sap.

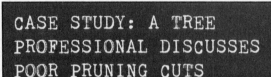

CASE STUDY: A TREE PROFESSIONAL DISCUSSES POOR PRUNING CUTS

Steve Pirus is a WSU Master Gardener and Certified Arborist in Vancouver, Washington, and he is also a member of the International Society of Arboriculture.

The first rule to remember in order to avoid a poor pruning job is never prune when the tree is stressed or during extreme high heat, drought, or severe freezing weather. And second, we do not cut a branch without a reason. Know what and why ahead of time.

For example, crown reduction is the reduction of diameter and, therefore, of the height and width of the crown of a tree. An arborist never tops a tree. Topping or hard-heading back, reducing the size of the crown, or greatly reducing the diameter of the tree encourages decay — or dying back — of the cuts, which can eventually die back into the trunk, slowly killing the tree. If you are going to do this, you should limit this to 25 to 30 percent of the live branches in any one year. An unskilled pruner will cut the same length of material from all the branches. A skilled arborist will remove, on a 20-foot-diameter tree, 12 inches from some branches, 18 inches, 24 inches, and 36 inches judiciously from various branches, leaving a more natural and pleasing look.

Having said this, the International Society of Arboriculture strongly recommends no crown reduction or attempts at limiting size. Certain professionals, including two major amusement parks in California and Florida, along with myself and other highly skilled individuals, will use this technique thoughtfully, on a yearly basis, to limit tree size. Picture a 30-plus-feet-in-diameter, established tree in a fixed location; without using this technique, the owner would have to remove a large, attractive, and well-established tree at a large expense in time and money. Then the owner would have to replace it with a significantly smaller tree that would not fulfill the landscape design requirement needed in that space.

Also, you may also thin out a tree to help prevent failure during high winds; this would be crown thinning, removing about 25 to 30 percent of the foliage at any one time but not more. If you remove too much foliage, the tree often responds by sending up fast, new, weak growth or sprout production, rather than slower, normal, more woody growth. So do not get too carried away.

Another poor pruning cut to avoid is to never cut off, or within, or violate the branch bark ridge because the cut cannot heal properly. The emphasis is placed on the proper branch bark ridge cut, but if you cannot see it, you should always make an angled cut outside the branch collar. A cut that violates the branch bark ridge is called a flush cut, and in basic terms, it reflects the work of an unskilled laborer — or tree criminal.

You also should avoid a technique called lion tailing. This is the removal of most of the foliage along a branch's length, leaving a portion 10, 15, or maybe 20 percent at the end of the branch. This leaves too much weight at the very end of the branch to swing in the wind and probably break off and not enough foliage along the length of the branch to feed it through photosynthesis.

Perhaps most importantly, always use the correct tool for the job. If you use the wrong tool, you will not have a clean cut, and you open the plant up to disease and insect infestation. The bottom line is, when approaching a pruning job, the correct approach is to accentuate or complement the natural character of each plant. Do not attempt to force them into some sort of contrived form you imagine but instead accentuate their beauty.

If you want to know the most important skills needed to prune properly and avoid poor pruning cuts and, thus, a poor pruning job, they are: always prune with clean, sharp tools, and know how to prune the branch bark ridge so you only remove branch tissue and you do not damage stem tissue. The rest is all window dressing.

— Chapter 6: —

Common Pruning Methods

You can easily get overwhelmed with the idea of pruning because overzealous pruning can harm the health of a plant. The best advice includes taking your pruning job slowly and remembering to continuously step back and observe your work. This will prevent over pruning and also give you a better perspective on what you hope to achieve. When in doubt, leave it alone — but do not be so afraid of pruning that you give up on the task. This chapter describes some basic pruning methods that anyone new to pruning can quickly learn and will give you confidence to move forward in your pruning.

Pinching

Pinching is an ongoing process for any gardener, and you perform it without tools: All you need is your thumb and forefinger. *As mentioned in Chapter 2, auxin, the chemical compound concentrated in the end of every branch, tells* *the plant to produce growth from that area.* The end bud always grows at the expense of the other buds growing on a branch or stem. In the case of a plant with opposite buds, the auxin level is the same in both end buds. If you want the plant to grow bushier and produce lower growth, you simply pinch off the actively growing end bud or buds. This forces the auxin level to rise in the lower buds, and they begin to grow. If the buds alternate with each other, pinching only one of the buds encourages the remaining bud to grow rather than generate growth of the lower buds.

You should know what type of plant you are working with before you start pinching. Plants, such as tulips, lilies, or other bulb plants where a single flowering stem constitutes the entire plant, should not be pinched. Other flowering plants, such as flowering annuals, produce more blooms and stronger plants when they are pinched back at 6 to 8 weeks of age. For example, snapdragons, marigolds, zinnias, and cosmos all generate more branches below the pinched area and produce more flowers. Pinching back flowering plants also helps the plants withstand adverse weather conditions. Although you pinch plants when they are young, pinching can be continuous process, such as when flowering plants are **deadheaded**, which is another name for removing old blooms. Occasionally, when you buy a plant, you will see instructions with it that tell you to give something a hard pinch, which takes off more than just the end bud and is done with a hand shear if the stem is too thick for a simple hand pinch.

Commercial cut flower growers use a different pinching process that can be expensive and cumbersome for the average gardener. They grow flowers for the florist trade using pinching to produce fewer and larger flowers per plant. They aim to produce the largest flower possible, even if this means the plant produces fewer flowers. To do this, the growers pinch lateral growth from some flowering plants like carnations or alstroemeria, removing all but a few of the best blooms. Commercial growers allow flowering plants like snapdragons and delphiniums, which produce only a single bloom, to grow tall without the competition from multiple blooms and extra foliage that would occur if they were not pinched at an early age. In this case, they use pinching to create large and outstanding blooms rather than stronger plants with numerous flowers. But, as a consequence of forcing the plants to make unnaturally sized blooms with extra long stems, field-grown plants grown by commercial growers are more prone to wind damage. To remedy this situation, most cut flower growers add support — using netting or stakes — to their plants.

You can pinch plants in the garden anytime during the growing season, meaning you can remove water sprouts and suckers as soon as you spot them. By doing this, you can save your tree from health problems and avoid a more complicated removal process. Also, you can pinch back tomato plants to three of four main stems to promote tomato growth. This helps eliminate wayward growth prone to aphid attacks.

Herbs that are commonly used for cooking — basil, oregano, marjoram, mint, lemon balm, coriander, dill, parsley, and thyme — benefit greatly from occasional pinching. Pinching forces the plants to grow more leaves and prevents the plants from blooming and going to seed. When these culinary herbs bloom, the taste of the essential oils change as the plants expend more energy producing blooms and seeds rather than more leaf growth. You can pinch back all culinary herbs further than just the tip end. Culinary herbs help attract beneficial insects, such as ladybugs and dragonflies. Beneficial insects prey on plant-damaging insects, such as aphids and caterpillars, and help pollinate your garden.

You can pinch all non-woody flowering perennials that die to the ground each winter early in the season to produce sturdier plants. A few examples of flowering perennials that respond well to pinching include Turk's cap (*Malvaviscus drummondii*), Mexican mint marigold (*Tagetes lucida*), and the shrimp plant (*Justicia brandegeana*). Simply pinch out the top green growth when the plants are about 6 inches high. Keep in mind that a plant will grow sturdier and thicker after you pinch it but not as tall.

Pinching chrysanthemums

If you have ever wondered how professional growers create those bushel-sized chrysanthemums they sell every fall, you can do it yourself because the procedure is simple. Start the chrysanthemum plant indoors from a cutting or root division as early as possible in the spring. Once all danger of frost has passed, plant the chrysanthemum in the garden in full sunlight and rich garden soil. Make sure the plant is located away from artificial lighting, such as porch lights, because chrysanthemums are sensitive to light levels when it comes to setting flower buds. Fertilize with a full-strength, water-soluble fertilizer every two weeks throughout the growing season.

Sometime during the first part of summer, you will see flower buds beginning to form. Pinch off the buds as they appear using your hand or a pair of hand shears. This process is called **debudding** and will cause your plant to produce fewer but larger blooms rather than many smaller blooms. Do not allow the buds to show color or open. You should end up with a nicely rounded specimen. If the shape is a little off, take a pair of manual shears, and make a few adjustments. Only cut the amount needed to remove all the flower buds and shape the plant. Continue to fertilize and water as required, and you will see the chrysanthemum grow into a nice bushel. In late summer, when you see the second round of blooms begin to form, stop fertilizing, but continue to keep the soil evenly moist, and enjoy the fall show once the blooms open. After the plant freezes, cut the dead foliage back to the ground. If desired, this is a good time for separating the roots for new plants to put out the following spring.

Shearing

Shearing is a pruning process used on hedges and evergreens where you redirect growth and remove unwanted leaves and branches. This stimulates dormant buds among the inner branches and nudges them to grow into a thick, bushy appearance. The best time to shear is a few days after plant growth starts; for most plants, this is in late spring. Shearing at this time allows you to effectively redirect new growth. This will curtail the growth of the end buds and form new buds where you make the cuts. Maintaining a hedge or shaped evergreen can be time consuming. If you shear your hedges to a formal style, it will require constant shearing to maintain their shape. If you have more informal, natural-looking hedges, you will still need to shear them a few times a year to stimulate flowering and to keep the foliage dense. If you live in a cold climate, stop any pruning six weeks before you expect fall frost because any new shoots need time to harden and gain strength to withstand winter weather. Properly maintained hedges can last for years.

Root Pruning

If you are a gardener, you know that the roots of a plant form the foundation of any plant and should never be bothered. You water them, mulch over them, and do whatever you need to do to keep them thriving. **Root pruning** involves cutting back the roots of a plant, much like you would when pruning parts of the plant above ground. In some situations, roots, just like the other portions of a plant, need pruning or reduction in size. Examples of these instances include preparing a plant for transplanting, slowing the growth of the plant, forcing blooms and fruit production, and keeping a container plant healthy.

Moving large plants

The procedure a plant nursery uses for removing trees grown in the ground for later sale is the same one you need to follow if you are going to move a large plant or shrub. It might be impossible to transport a 6-foot-tall or larger tree with all the roots intact. The roots may extend 5 feet or more in every direction. Furthermore, the amount of dirt needed to keep the roots covered would be heavy. Root pruning keeps the plant healthy if moved. The root system of a plant has feeder roots that form toward the outer ends of the root system, and if you suddenly cut all the roots of a tree and dig it up, the tree has no way to take up moisture and nutrients when planted in the new location.

You should perform root pruning to prepare a large bush for transplanting during the winter or late fall while the plant is dormant. This takes careful planning. If you move a bush without properly preparing it, the plant will suffer and may die. One year before digging the plant from the ground, you should use a shovel with a long, sharp blade or a mechanical blade to slice half the roots off at a certain distance from the tree. The distance depends on the size of the tree and the method of transportation, but for the 6-foot-tree example, you would work in a circle 10 inches from the trunk of the tree. Large machinery can dig and remove a large tree with the entire root ball intact, but if you are moving by hand or using lighter machinery, you will have to work closer to the tree. The theory behind root pruning is that once you cut the roots, numerous feeder roots will form at the ends of where you pruned. When the tree is dug the following winter, the chance of transplant shock is lessened considerably because there are established roots in place.

In the year before you move the bush, prune the roots by cutting all of the roots in a half circle around the plants, or prune by marking the circle around the plant into four sections and cut one-quarter of the roots on opposite sides of the circle. Another method is to use the blade to make a cut, and then skip a space the size of the blade, and make another cut. You should give extra moisture to the tree throughout the growing season because you reduced the root ball, but be careful not to add too much water because it could drown or rot. You make the rest of the cuts the next dormant season when the tree or shrub is pulled from the ground to sell or transplant. Since the new feeder roots form at the end of the pruned roots, you must dig the plant up at least 6 inches away from where you pruned the roots.

When properly pruned, a transplanted shrub or tree's roots will quickly heal and send out **hair roots**, which are smaller roots that grow from established plant roots. They increase the amount of surface area the plant can reach for nutrients.

Slowing a plant's growth

You can root prune established trees to slow down the growth of the tree. You might think you can simply prune back a shrub or tree's branches. But because pruning branches causes shrubs and trees to grow new branches, this can cause the plant to grow even quicker.

Because a tree depends on a robust root system for healthy growth, pruning the roots slows down the tree's growth and can lead to dwarfing of the tree. If you drastically prune the roots, then you need to prune the top of the tree to compensate. This is the theory behind the art of bonsai. Although bonsai is an extreme example, trees and bushes can be dwarfed or have their growth slowed down at any stage of growth through careful root and crown pruning. *To learn more about bonsai, see Chapter 8.*

Forcing blooms and fruit production

Root pruning offers an effective means of controlling the growth of fruit and flowering trees and bushes. A fruit tree can grow for many years without producing any fruit. By pruning a plant's roots, you can force it to bear fruit or blooms. Also, root pruning is often done to encourage blooms on old perennial vines, such as wisteria or bougainvillea. The theory behind this method is the plant uses too much energy for root production at the expense of fruit or bloom production — in other words, the plant is too happy and needs a little stress to initiate blooms. After root pruning occurs, the plant takes up less nitrogen, which encourages flowering, not leaf growth. When it is not stressed by getting too much fertilizer or water, it only produces lush, green growth.

In this case, half to three-quarters of the roots are pruned in a circle 2 to 3 feet out from the base of the tree, vine, or shrub between the late fall and early spring. This is only a theory, and in some cases it does not work, but it should not do long-term damage to the plant if done correctly.

Root pruning container plants

Container plants, whether trees and shrubs you are preparing for transplant or plants grown in containers for the patio, often need root pruning to remain healthy. Also, you might notice a plant growing too large for its pot, which requires either having its growth limited or placing it in a new container.

If you choose to prune the roots of your container plant, you will take the plant from the container and see roots wrapped around each other, sometimes growing entirely around the root ball. These roots continue to grow in a circle, causing problems. Eventually, they become so thick, they surround the base of the tree, strangling it so moisture and nutrients cannot work their way up or down the tree through the normal transpiration process.

When a plant begins to grow too large for its pot, you can amend the situation in three ways. You can prune the roots and put the plant in the same pot; you can transplant the plant to a new container; or you can plant the shrub or tree in the ground. If you want to keep your plant in the same container, simply cut back all of the outside roots, and replant it in the container with new soil. This will save you from continually potting your plant in new containers. You need to do this once a year or every few years, depending on how quickly your plant grows. Once you put your tree or shrub back in its container, you will also need to prune the branches to keep the top part of the tree in proportion to the size of the pot.

If you are transplanting potted plants to a larger pot, you should follow the same method of cutting off encircling roots. If you are moving a plant from a larger to a smaller container, prune off enough roots so that the root ball is 1 inch from the sides of the new container. You should also prune off one-third of the top growth to compensate for the decrease in root mass.

When transplanting a tree or shrub for a pot into the ground, slide the plant out of the pot, and then slice the root ball with a knife in several places. Next, take your knife or a stick, and gently pull on the roots at the surface of the root ball. This encourages the roots to grow outward. If you cannot untangle some of the more tangled roots, make vertical slits in the root ball with your knife. This will encourage the plant to grow new feeder roots closer to the tree's drip line. **Feeder roots** are dense networks of roots spread close to the soil's surface that absorb most of the nutrients for the tree. A **drip line** is the area located directly under the outermost leaves of a tree. Encouraging roots to grow outward will help your plant stay healthy after transplantation.

When to avoid root pruning

People love their trees, but sometimes trees can cause problems — shallow tree roots buckle sidewalks, invade septic systems, or threaten building foundations. When this happens, the first reaction is to cut the offending root, but this can lead to the rapid decline of a mature tree. Because every situation is unique, you should consult a certified arborist for advice. The best way to avoid ever having to think about root pruning a mature tree is never planting shallow-rooted trees, such as cottonwoods, sycamores, or willows, close to a place they can cause trouble in the future. Most fast-growing trees and trees native to swampy or wet areas have a shallow root structure.

Sometimes, established trees and bushes will have roots that grow above the ground. These roots become exposed and make it difficult to mow or walk around the shrub. In addition to affecting the health of your tree, exposed roots can also affect the health of the grass and any ground covers around it. Some gardeners cover these roots by planting low bushes, like hostas, around or near trees to add visual interest to a garden. You may feel tempted to cover these roots with dirt or cut them out, but this can be disastrous to the tree and result in death to the top of the tree on the side where the roots were covered or damaged. Cutting the roots can also result in rot at the base of the tree. In addition, covering the roots with soil will reduce oxygen that roots need to survive. Once this happens, leaves may become discolored and fall prematurely, or you may begin to see dead branches on the tree. A better solution in dealing with exposed roots is to simply leave them alone. You can cut a bed around the tree, and then cover the exposed roots with mulch. It may not be your ideal solution, but it will keep your tree's root system healthy.

Chapter 7

Other Pruning Methods

You do not have to be a professional to create some of the many artistic shapes you may know through pruning. It takes work, and it also requires constant maintenance, but it can add a fun and creative dimension to your pruning and gardening.

Pollarding

Pollarding is a type of pruning also known as tree shaping that creates a manicured look. You can see pollarded trees in various big American cities, such as San Francisco where there is an outstanding collection of pollarded trees in front of the San Francisco Civic Center and lining the streets in certain European cities. Pollarding began in medieval Great Britain and Europe when people cut tree limbs for basket and furniture making, for livestock food, and for firewood. The next season, they again harvested the profusion of fresh growth that grew from where they cut the limbs and so on. After many years, the subject tree developed huge clubby growths known as pollard heads on the end of the limbs where they harvested the smaller limbs every year. Instead of cutting the tree to the ground every year, the limbs were established on a taller tree to keep the new growth out of the reach of wildlife and domestic animals. If you have ever seen a pollarded tree, you cannot easily forget it. You either consider it an interesting work of art or a travesty. Pollarding differs from topping a tree because pollarding involves an ongoing process that begins when the tree is young. Topping involves a one time, stressful act done on a mature tree that can increase the chance for disease and weather-related injuries.

Pollarding establishes a framework of six to eight lateral or scaffold limbs on a fast-growing tree, such as a sycamore or willow. It involves cutting off the top of a tree and cutting the branches back to the trunk so that in summer, a mass of shoots burst out of the head or heads. You determine the eventual height of the scaffold limbs, as pollarding is not an exact science. You can train the tree to grow the limbs in a spiral arrangement. Remove any side branches growing from the limbs. When you reach the desired number of scaffold limbs and the desired height of the tree, cut off the leader branch in the center of the tree. Every year or two during the dormant season, cut off all the growth that appeared the previous season, and shorten the limbs so they are 2 to 5 feet from the trunk. Because the beauty of a pollarded tree is in the interesting leafless and clubby scaffolding limbs, prune early in the dormant season so you can enjoy your creation. Good trees for pollarding include sycamores, willows, ashes, maples, and mulberries.

Coppicing

Coppicing could be considered the low-growing cousin of pollarding. It is simply the process of cutting down a fast-growing deciduous tree or large shrub to within 6 inches of the ground and allowing multiple stems to come up in place of the trunk. Once again, people did this to create multiple smaller limbs for weaving, livestock food, and fuel. The main difference between coppicing and pollarding is that coppicing is used for wildlife management. In forests where tall tree canopies shade out any growth on the forest floor, a tree can be cut at the base rather than completely removed. This allows sunlight to reach the forest floor, and the coppiced tree also provides tender growth for animals, such as deer and rabbit, to browse. Coppicing is an ongoing process that you must continue after starting on a large scale. If people coppice too many trees in a wooded area, eventually the forest will have many small limbs coming up everywhere that restrict wildlife movement. The stump left after tree coppicing is known as a "stool." Both coppicing and pollarding can extend the lives of trees for hundreds of years.

Pleaching

Pleaching is a curious example of pruning and training a tree or shrub. When pleaching, a series of woody plants are planted close enough together that their limbs can touch or are at least planted close enough so the trees can be bent over and woven together. If a tree is braided through another tree, or pleached, eventually the trees will grow together. Trees can be pleached at a high level so they create a canopy or a two-dimensional wall of growth if carefully pruned. Young trees can be bent over a walkway or path and pleached so they form a green tunnel. There is really no limit to what can be done when it comes to pleaching. Although time consuming, it is a creative and fun activity. Choose the plants you are going to pleach carefully. You want to choose trees with flexible limbs not covered with a thick layer of bark early in life. Linden and sycamore are good choices for a large project, and yaupon holly and ficus trees are good choices for a smaller project. They grow fast, and you can see results in a few years rather than decades. Any sized yard or garden will do because pleaching is simply a matter of growing two or more trees together.

The history of pleaching

The Romans invented the art of pleaching trees, and Julius Caesar used them as a military obstacle. During this time, people also used pleaching to encourage new growth on trees, as well as prevent damage to new trees during flooding.

During medieval times, people performed pleaching horizontally — rather than vertically — because they used it as protection against annual flooding but not as a protector against damage to new trees. Rather, pleached trees created a connected, raised space about 8 feet above flood waters, and on this space, people constructed huts that protected them against the elements.

To build this space, they planted trees of the same species in a grid-like formation, similar to how orchards are planted. As the saplings grew, they pruned branches and trained them to grow toward a neighboring tree like a graft. As trees merged with other trees, they also combined their life systems of water, minerals, and sap. Once the grafted branches matured into large limbs, they had the strength to hold the weight of planks that they laid on top, as well as the huts they then built on the planks. Foliage from the outer trees sheltered the huts from the elements and may have even provided fruit to eat.

Also during medieval times, pleaching gained popularity for use in formal gardens. In fact, the word "pleach" derives from the old French word "plechier," meaning to braid or intertwine. During the Middle Ages and through to the mid-18th century, many formal gardens, first in France and then later in England and other royal European gardens, contained walkways and pleached structures. Pleaching was, in fact, a status symbol because in order to maintain the design, the landowner had to employ many gardeners, which meant that he had the money to do so.

As time passed, farmers also used pleaching to make boundary hedges more secure. When pleaching hedges, the technique is called hedgelaying. *Hedgelaying is discussed in further detail in Chapter 11.*

How to pleach

One of the fun things about pleaching is that there are several ways you can set up your canvas: as a singular row where trees or hedges intertwine, as two rows facing each other to create an archway or a tunnel along a walkway, or as trees planted in a square or circle to create a pleached canopied ceiling or room.

Make sure you choose trees that have strong, yet flexible branches, such as apple, pear, fig, beech, hornbeam, olive, linden, willow, almond, sycamore, wisteria, lime, or dogwood. You must choose trees of the same species and of similar size and variety. Spacing will depend on what you want to pleach — that is, whether you want to form an archway, tunnel, or canopy — but make sure you space the saplings equally. This can range from 2 to 10 feet apart or more.

Next, stake the trees into the ground about 3 feet, with the top of the stakes reaching as high as the top growth. You will also need horizontal batons — such as canes, wires, or wooden posts — with cross pieces for tying in and training the side branches until they grow into each other. You will eventually remove this framework, but you need it initially for support and for directing growth into the shape you desire.

Start by tying in a side shoot — one shoot on the right and one shoot on the left — to each horizontal support. Choose shoots just below the side supports so they must arch up rather than bend down. Then, take the topmost shoot and bend it toward the tree you want it to intertwine with; tie this to the support of that tree you want to intertwine it with. The direction of the bend will vary depending on whether you want a row, tunnel, or canopy. Occasionally, head off or cut this main shoot to stimulate growth in the side shoots.

Although you will eventually want a smooth lower trunk reaching from the ground to your pleached branches, you should initially allow some of the lower branches to grow on each young tree — this helps thicken the trunk. But, make sure to pinch these temporary branches back to less than 1 foot long, and cut them off completely after a few years.

Once the branches from the trees grow so they reach each other, you can then weave them together or tie them together. If you tie them together, you must eventually remove this tie, or it will strangle the branches. Cut off any branches growing perpendicular to the plane of the pleached trees.

Once your trees have successfully filled the desired area, you must prune them annually from top to bottom. Also, remove any stems growing up from the ground area or along any of the branches. If some of the growth is too dense, make sure to thin it out to allow light to penetrate.

Eventually, you will need to remove your support frame. This will occur when your pleached trees are sturdy and the branches have naturally grafted or grown together. Once this happens, the support systems of the trees will merge their life processes of water, minerals, and sap.

You can also pleach hedges, commonly known in Europe as hedgelaying. Hedgelaying is similar to tree pleaching because each hedge is grafted to the hedge next to it to form a boundary.

First, you cut each stem or trunk along the hedge near the ground, leaving enough upper branches to allow sap flow to keep the hedge alive. When deciding how many upper branches to leave, use caution. You do not want the top to look bare. Next, place a row of vertical stakes in the ground to hold the hedge upright. Then, intertwine the branches of the hedge along the line of the hedge.

The next step involves weaving long, flexible lengths of hazel strands along the top of the hedge and between the stakes — to keep the hedge sturdy. Then, trim the hedge, and leave it until the next pruning season. At that time, you will cut any new growth that has occurred to promote thickening and to create an A-shaped cross section, wherein the branches are pruned so that the new top growth forms an A shape. This allows light to penetrate the center of the hedge to encourage new growth to create a thicker, denser hedge.

Crown Raising

Crown raising — also called crown lifting or raising the skirt — is cutting off the bottom limbs of a tree or large shrub. It is the opposite of **crown reduction** — when a tree has grown too large for its intended space. It also is different from **crown thinning** — when branches are pruned throughout the crown to allow light to penetrate and air to move throughout the crown or upper story or canopy of the tree. Certain trees, such as pine trees, go through a natural pruning process where the bottom limbs have so much shade they die and fall off. A pine tree may be 20 years old before it has enough limbs naturally removed to offer shade to a person sitting or standing under its branches.

Crown raising is done for a number of reasons. One of the most common reasons is to create space under a tree for people, vehicles, buildings, or other trees, shrubs, and plants. For example, in parks, crown raising can create space for people to park their vehicles, sit, or walk under trees.

Public safety reasons also prompt crown raising around buildings and roads. For example, when trees line a street or highway, people will remove lower branches so drivers can see the road in both good and bad weather. It can eliminate branches from obstructing not only the roads but also traffic lights and road signs. On roads and driveways, crown raising is necessary to allow for headroom of passing and parked cars, and when vehicles are parked, to allow for passengers to get in and out of their cars. Crown raising can allow for greater visual access, preventing traffic or pedestrian accidents. When trees grow too close to buildings or windows, crown raising can prevent branches from obstructing light into a room or building, or it can prevent safety issues like branches falling on the roof.

Crown raising is also used in forest management — lower branches are removed to increase the amount of timber produced and the quality of the wood. This happens by concentrating knots into a small interior core of trunk wood, providing early formation of clear, knot-free timber. Because frequency, size, and knot types determine the value of lumber, crown raising is one way to increase the cost and quality of timber.

Crown raising also gets rid of decayed wood or diseased parts of the tree that can weaken the health of a tree. Certain trees are susceptible to disease of the lower trunk, and crown raising can be used as a preventative measure against diseases. For example, pruned white pines can avoid a condition called white pine blister rust, which strikes lower branches of this species.

Crown raising can improve the look of a tree or allow access to pathways blocked from lower branches. If you desire to have a tree you can sit under, crown raising can provide the space. Crown raising can also allow light to penetrate trees, shrubs, or plants that grow below the tree or in the tree's shade coverage. In this case, crown lifting is beneficial to the health of other trees and plants in the yard or garden.

How to "raise the skirt"

Crown raising is a simple procedure when the lower branches of the crown or canopy of the tree are removed. The trick is to not overdo it because it can cause stress, damage, or death to the tree.

You should only prune the lower branches to the point of providing enough clearance for people, vehicles, or other vegetation. When you complete crown raising, the remaining crown of the tree should be two-thirds of the height of the tree so the crown and tree as a whole remains balanced in height and appearance.

To achieve this, you need to remember that what you do on one side of the lower part of the tree should be done on the other. Make sure you cut an equal amount of branches from each side of the tree to preserve the proportion of the tree. Unless the job requires a higher clearance, only remove branches from the ground to the desired height of the lowest secondary branch.

To prevent these problems, do what nature does and take off a little at a time by following the same formula as you do for newly planted trees: Take off an area one-fifth of the tree's height each year until you obtain the desired height. For a 60-foot tree, you can remove 12 feet of growth, which is plenty to create an enjoyable space. But, for a smaller tree only 20 feet high, take off only 4 feet, and wait until the next pruning season to remove another 4 feet. Only take off as much as needed when basal pruning so that you never prune off a total amount of limbs that equal a space greater than one-third of the tree's height. When this happens, the top section of the tree becomes too heavy in relation to the rest of the tree, and the tree can snap in half in high winds.

The ration of live crown to total tree height should be at least two-thirds. Image courtesy of the USDA.

A few words of caution: Crown raising should not include the removal of large branches growing directly out of the tree's trunk. Removing large branches opens up wounds in the tree that can lead to decay or insect infestation, jeopardizing the future health of the tree. In cases where you cannot avoid the removal of these branches — such as the tree's heavy branches are the ones that need removal in order to create the space desired — you should remember the recovery time for the tree will be longer. To help preserve the health of the tree, you can also prune off one-third of the limb the first year, and the next year when you prune the tree, you can remove the remainder of the limb. This gives the tree the time to adjust for the loss. A rule of thumb is that if the diameter of a limb is greater than half the diameter of the tree, you should remove it in stages. Remove these heavy branches in three or four pieces to make the job easier and safer. It might be preferable to use a mechanical lift rather than a ladder.

Some useful tips to remember when crown raising include:

- Try not to go overboard when removing these branches because this could lead to the development of a top-heavy tree.

- When cutting back to the trunk, do not forget to use the three-step method of using an undercut first to prevent stripping of the trunk.

- Use caution and be conservative when selecting which branches to remove. Limit the size and number of branches as much as possible, and keep the removal well spaced.

- Keep in mind that crown lifting introduces light to the bottom part of the tree, which can encourage growth from dormant buds. To thwart this from happening, leave smaller branches on the lower part of the trunk. This will **trunk taper**, meaning the tree trunk will decrease in diameter with height, and it will also protect the tree from the being harmed by the sun. Keep these temporary branches about 4 to 6 inches apart along the stem. Make sure they are pruned annually and eventually removed.

- The most favorable time to perform crown lifting is during the late summer, when branches are at their fullest in foliage and can give you a better view of what needs removal.

- Also, you might want to consult an arborist before embarking on this project because the lower branches play an important role in how a tree sways in high winds and storms.

Drop-crotching

Drop-crotching — also referred to as crown reduction — is a way to selectively thin out a tree so the basic shape of the tree remains. Occasionally, because of poor pruning methods or storm damage, the crown needs redefining. For example, a fruit tree may become too top heavy because of previous pruning to encourage fruit growth. Also, drop-crotching can thin out a tree to increase light penetration and air movement throughout the crown of the tree. Shearing or topping the tree is not considered an acceptable way to reduce the crown area. On mature trees, you should consult a professional for reducing the crown area.

The process of drop-crotching removes branches from the crown of the tree because they are too long or too high. Each branch is cut back to a fork in the tree called a **crotch**. The forks are branches that have a live branch at least half the width of the branch being pruned, or they are the main stem. In this method of pruning, the branches are shortened over the entire main branch system of the tree. Every place where you see a branch grow out of a bigger limb is a crotch. They can be located anywhere in the tree, from the highest point to the lower canopy.

When drop-crotching, you should keep a balanced shape so you should not thin or reduce more than 25 percent of the crown. Keep the cut as close to the parent branch as possible. Keep in mind that severe drop-crotching will stress the tree and lower its natural defense system because of the large wounds that result in the places where the branches have been pruned. Drop-crotching is preferable to stub cuts, where you do not prune up to the collar or trunk of the tree, because drop-crotch wounds are closer to the stem and heal more quickly. Within a few months, sprouts will grow in the places you cut so you must also prune these because these new growths will tend to be weakly attached and unsafe.

The proper way to prune is to make sure you position all cuts just above a substantial branch, and you make these cuts over the entire main branch system for balance. When thinning, remove branches off substantial or main branches. Do not cut the main branches themselves

To prevent branch die back, cuts should be made at lateral branches that are at least one-third the diameter of the stem at their union. Image courtesy of the USDA.

unless necessary, as in the case of branches touching power lines, roofs, sides, or windows of buildings. Choose those stems or branches that form a V-shape attachment to the substantial branch that is being thinned. Be sure to remove the whole length of the selected stem branches, and cut as close to the parent branch as possible.

Begin your cut on the underside of the branch you are pruning, well up from the V-crotch. For these cuts, use a pointed bow saw if the limb is thin or hard to reach, and use a D-shaped bow saw if the limb is thicker or heavier. Next, make your second cut on the top side of the branch, from the inside of the crotch but well up from the initial cut and the ridge of bark that joins the two branches. Be sure to cut all the way through the branch so only the stub remains. Next, shorten this stub by making your final cut just to one side of the branch bark ridge and parallel to it.

Leave branches that form a U-shape of attachment. Also avoid forming **lion tails**, which are tufts of foliage and branches at the end of branches caused by removing all inner lateral branches and foliage. If you leave the lion tails, you risk sun scalding on branches and the trunk, as well as **epicormic sprouting,** which are shoots growing on the mature section of the main stem, trunk, or branch. Lion tails can also result in weak branch structure and breakage. Always remove branches that rub against or cross other branches.

The best time of year to drop-crotch is during late fall or winter. During the dormant season, there is less sap loss, which means less stress to the tree. Also, fungi and insects also tend to be dormant during the late fall and winter, meaning the opportunity for infection or infestation is not as high. And because deciduous trees are leafless during this time, you can see the shape of the tree and the branches that need thinning better. You should always remove dead branches, no matter what time of the year.

You should thin as little as necessary rather than harm the tree by over thinning.

Creating a Standard for Trees and Bushes

When professional gardeners — those who make their living from taking care of trees and plants — talk about creating a **standard**, they are referring to training a bushy plant to have a clear, upright stem and a rounded cotton ball-shaped top, like those trees drawn in children's picture books.

When certified arborists — professionals who have studied arboriculture, or the cultivation, management, and study of trees — talk about creating a standard with trees and bushes, they are talking about following the pruning rules set by the American National Standards Institute (ANSI). These include adhering to definite instructions on how to prune various trees and shrubs and what tools to use for each individual job, as well as how to take care of and clean pruning tools so that disease is not spread. This book mentions these same guidelines, and you can find them online at **www.ansi.org**.

Gardeners and arborists both love and hate standards, depending on personal preferences, but those who advocate creating standards usually do it for fun. You are pretty much creating a miniature lollipop-looking tree, and it is fairly easy to do.

How to create a standard

You can create a standard with a seedling, a rooted cutting, or an established bushy plant. Keep in mind, young plants are more flexible than established ones, and their rapid growth makes them easier to train to a standard form because you are not fighting against years of old growth. Also, with a young plant, there is less risk of damaging, stunting, or even killing the plant.

If you are using a seedling or rooted cutting, select a plant that has a strong center stem or branch. If you are using an established plant, choose one that has a larger central branch, and lop off all stems down to the soil level. You should note that pruning off all the lower branches can stress an older, established bush, which might make it a poor candidate for creating a standard. Leave plenty of branches and leaves on the top part of the center stem so the plant can produce enough energy to sustain itself and grow in a healthy way.

Next, place a stake in the soil, and tie the main center stem of your seedling, rooted cutting, or bushy plant to the stake every few inches. The stakes ensure the eventual trunk will grow straight, and upright growth consumes more of the plant's energy so this should also help to suppress the growth of lower buds. Once the plant matures or reaches full height and the central stem is strong, you can remove the stake. A mature plant will be dense with fully-grown leaves. Removing the stake is your call, but you can tell if the main stem is ready by whether it appears strong and upright. If there are any shoots growing near the base of the plant, remove them. Most of these shoots will not grow back if they are cut off when the plant is still young.

In the second year of growth, some branches may begin to grow from the main stem, and you should pinch them back to weaken them. Do this every time the plant grows a few inches. Continue to prune off any branches growing below the bushy top growth of the rounded top. Also, occasionally clip the top growth. This will encourage more growth from the top of your center leader.

One area of concern if you live in a climate with harsh winters: Standard trees are less hardy in winter than if they had remained bushy shrubs because they are missing their side branches. If your standard plant is in a planter, you can easily bring it indoors when the weather is cold. But, if your standard tree is in the ground, be sure to insulate the stem with a burlap bag.

Choosing your standard

Two kinds of standard trees exist: **ornamental standards** and **standards**. Both are small, but ornamentals are dwarf sized — or smaller than usual — and are usually in pots.

Creating standards is increasingly popular because it is a fun way to enjoy the beauty of a tree without the space required for many traditional trees. This is especially true when creating ornamental or tree standards in large containers, although many standards do just as well when planted in the ground. Containers give you the freedom of bringing your standard indoors in cold weather, which is an advantage when dealing with plants, such as rosemary and citrus, which can die when the thermometer dips.

There are endless choices of plants that make great standards, but here are some favorites among gardeners:

Rosemary is a favorite choice as a dwarf-sized standard, often growing no more than 2 feet tall. The rosemary foliage is a semi-evergreen silver and green, which produces small blue flowers in summer. Rosemary leaves are decorative, and they also have a functional use: Rosemary is a popular herb used to season meat, sauces, and soup. Rosemary does best when grown in pots and moved indoors if you live in a climate with cold winters.

Dwarf orange trees are another great choice when growing an ornamental standard. If you live in a cold-winter climate, it is especially important to grow dwarf oranges in containers you can take indoors. Pinch off some of the fruit buds so the tree can keep its lollipop, rounded form. The tree will still bear fruit on the remaining buds.

Ornamental cherry trees can be grown in the ground and provide three separate interesting seasons: spring with its cherry blossoms, summer with its cherry fruit, and fall with its interesting colors of yellow, orange, and brown. But, these trees can reach a height of 10 to 15 feet so you should do some pruning each year to maintain the standard rounded form.

Camellias are a type of evergreen shrubs and small trees, originally native to Asia, that make another great choice for standard trees. Camellias have shiny leaves and showy, rose-like blooms that come in red, white, and pink. In both cherry and camellia plants, select a young plant with a strong center stem. Remove the lower foliage and any shoots along the stem. Stake the main stem, and once it reaches the height you desire, pinch off the tip growth. This will force the plant to branch out, creating the rounded top you desire. Camellias are hardy shrubs and do well both in the ground and in containers. They prefer partial shading and do well as an ornamental plant or along fences or walls.

Gardenias are a favorite type of garden shrub; they are known for their snow-white blooms that pop against their dark green leaves. But, their strong scent attracts many gardeners. The finicky gardenia prefers mild, cooler temperatures, about 62 degrees Fahrenheit, as well as humidity. This dual need can make it difficult to keep them from drooping and dropping their blooms if you have them in your house. The challenge — especially in winter — is to find a place in your home cooler than the rest of your house, yet humid. Bathrooms or a laundry room are two rooms that might provide cool, humid environments. Although gardenias can survive without pruning, annual clipping can keep the bush shapely and attractive and at the size you prefer. Gardenias do well as ornamental shrubs and also as large bushes. A shrub can be pruned on old and new wood alike but will bloom regardless of whether or not it is pruned.

Rose bushes in their many different types can easily be trained to grow as standards. Be sure to select a **re-blooming** or **ever-blooming** variety, a plant that will bloom several times a year as opposed to one that only blooms once a year so you can enjoy beautiful roses all season; some rose varieties have short blooming seasons. Remove dead blooms, and prune branches in the early spring to keep the tree looking its best. Roses do not do well if pruned when weather is cool or cold so wait until you see new growth on your shrub before clipping. Only cut back a ¼-inch above a bud, and always leave two healthy leaves on the stem to ensure that the plant remains strong. Rose bushes can do well as ornamental plants, but some varieties can also grow up to 10 feet tall. Also, make sure your rose bush receives adequate sunlight because roses need six hours of sunlight a day. This sunlight should be morning sun as opposed to afternoon sun because rose bush leaves are prone to mildew, and the morning sun will dry the dew that causes mold and other fungi diseases.

Hibiscus makes an excellent standard plant because its large, woody shrubs are easy to train. These plants come in a wide variety of bloom colors and can live in different climates. Some hibiscus varieties can withstand cold climates, while others cannot survive low temperatures. If you live in a cooler climate and you choose a variety sensitive to the cold, keep it in a container to bring indoors during the winter season.

Bougainvilleas present an interesting challenge as a standard tree because they are vines and need intense heat. In fact, they need at least five hours of sunlight a day. You must grow bougainvillea in a pot or container because it is sensitive to the cold, and it must have some kind of support. One way to support the plant involves creating a braided trunk. Start by choosing three bougainvilleas only a few inches in height with only a few, if any, side branches. Next, fill a pot or container with soil, and put a stake in the center. Place the three plants evenly around the stake, as close to the stake as possible, and water well. Braid the plants around the stake until you reach the top of the stake. Cut off any remaining side branches, but leave two remaining branches at the end of each vine. As the vines grow, continue to braid the stems, and cut off any new side branches, but always leave the two branches at the end of each vine. When the vines reach the top of the stake, pinch the top growth tip of each vine. Leave at least three sets of leaves at the end of each vine. These will branch out and create your standard top. Since bougainvilleas grow fast, you can create your standard tree in as little as 2 to 2 ½ years. Some varieties that make excellent standard trees include Barbara Karst, San Diego, superstition gold, torch glow, Jamaica red, violet, and double orange pink.

Topiaries

Topiary is the art of creating sculptures out of trees and shrubs by means of careful pruning. These include geometric forms, arches, animals, or any shape you can come up with. Its origins date back to the Roman era, but it became a popular garden art form in England during the Renaissance period. It fell out of favor in the 18th century but enjoyed a revival in the mid-1800s. In 1962, Walt Disney brought topiaries back in favor when he used them in his creations of Disneyland® and Disney World®. Topiaries have never been as popular in the United States as they are in Europe, but for creative-minded people, they can add an interesting aspect to the garden.

You can create topiaries in any size, making them interesting and fun. Shapes and sizes are only limited by your imagination, although artistic skill definitely helps. People often use trees and shrubs like evergreens with small leaves or needles for topiaries, although you can use some deciduous trees, which is discussed further in this chapter. A pruned hedge is a form of topiary in perhaps its simplest form.

You can get creative when pruning bushes. Geometric-shaped bushes like these add an interesting element to a garden.

The ideal plant to choose as a topiary grows slowly and tolerates repeated pruning without suffering any stress.

You should also choose one capable of re-sprouting from older wood and hardy enough to withstand the cold.

How to create your topiary

You should plant the plant or plants you choose for your topiary in an area that receives full sun. The tree or shrub needs to receive light on all sides or the sculpture will have bare parts and holes. Start by shaping your plant when it is young — although you can create topiaries from older, dense, overgrown plants, but training at this stage is more difficult. To make your job easier, especially if you have never created topiary before, you may want to create a frame from wire or wood that you form into the desired shape of your topiary. If you choose not to use a frame, make sure you prune slowly, and step back from time to time to examine your shape. Begin pruning as soon as any growth starts, and continue to shear throughout the summer. If you are using an evergreen as your topiary, you will probably only need to shear it two to three times a year. If you are using a deciduous plant, you may need to prune more often — these grow faster than evergreens. Clip all around the tree or shrub, and remove any unwanted branches between the sculpted areas. It is a good idea to keep the heaviest shapes toward the bottom of plant so it does not become top heavy and stressed from the weight.

Once your topiary is fully grown and is sculpted to your desired shape, you will need to prune it one to three times a year, depending on the plant you have chosen. If you live in a colder climate, prune your topiary at midsummer to lessen the chances of your pruning stimulating re-growth before spring of the following year. If you live in a warm climate, do it at the coolest time of the year so the sun does not scald the newly pruned wounds.

Types of topiaries

You can create three types of topiary: a topiary made from vines, a topiary made from a shrub or tree, and a topiary made by combining two or more plants into a desired sculpture.

Vine topiary is created when vines are allowed to grow on top of an already existing topiary. Choose a plant that grows in vines, such as an English ivy or Boston ivy, and make sure your vine grows quickly and tolerates changing conditions.

You may want to first fill in your shape with sphagnum moss, a genus of moss made up of 350 different species that is sometimes called peat moss, to make your topiary look fuller. You can find sphagnum moss growing in the wild, but you can also purchase it at some nurseries or on the Internet. After you have created your topiary form, plant the vine around the form. This allows the vine to grow up the form. Vine topiary can grow out of the ground or in a pot or container. As the vines grow, train it by wrapping it around the form. Prune or pinch back any growths from the vine that you cannot train. You will end up with an attractive and unique topiary.

Creating topiary from a shrub or tree is a little more difficult than when you use a vine to grow over and around an existing topiary. Your best choice is to use a juvenile shrub as opposed to one fully grown, but you can do the latter, too, although an older shrub is more difficult to train. If your shrub is in the ground, it will require more time and patience than if it is in a container. Start by trimming off no more than 1 to 3 inches to create your desired shape. This will prevent you from trimming too many leaves, and it will also encourage additional growth that will help your shrub become bushier or denser. Also, taking more than 3 inches could cause parts of the shrub to go into shock and die. Every three months or so, when there is active growth, continue to train and prune. Even after your topiary is the desired form, you will need to continue to prune new growth to keep the desired shape.

Using a metal or wooden frame creates topiary from a shrub more easily. Expert pruners often use frames because they make the job easier. You can buy a frame or make one yourself. Begin by pushing a stake or pole into the ground, as close as possible to the center of the plant. Next, secure the frame to a point on the stake to prevent the frame from shifting over time. Wait until new stems emerge from the frame, and then neatly clip them back. Should you want some stems to emerge from the frame in order to fill out the shape, tie those loosely to the frame with a twine that will biodegrade as the shrub grows.

Topiaries using more than one plant require careful planning. A frame is a must in creating this type of topiary. You can either plant two — or more — shrubs side by side or let one grow up inside and through the other to create your desired shape. You can use shrubs of the same type of plant or different plants to make the visual more interesting. This, of course, is a higher level of difficulty and will be more time consuming, especially when you consider that no matter how many plants you use in your topiary or how much training and pruning are involved, a plant will eventually go back to its natural growth pattern. As long as you do not mind maintaining your creation, a topiary offers a source of beauty and pleasure.

Choosing your plant

You can create topiaries from both evergreens and deciduous trees. Not all plants make good candidates for topiaries. Your best bets include plants that are slow-growing, are able to re-sprout from older wood, and are able to handle the stress of repeated pruning. Here are a few that work well as topiaries.

Boxwood

Evergreens make great topiaries because their needles or leaves make crisp, straight cuts and their leaves remain on the tree all year. A particularly popular evergreen often used as a topiary is the **boxwood**, a broadleaf evergreen desired for its rounded, bushy growth. A **broadleaf evergreen** has leaves instead of needles.

Boxwoods are one of the oldest plants used for ornamental uses, dating back to the Egyptians, Greeks, and then the Romans. In fact, ancient woodcarvings from China dating back to 1600 B.C. show pictures of boxwoods. They make excellent topiaries because of their denseness, hardiness, and longevity; plus, they are easy to grow. Boxwoods have shallow root systems, and you can easily transplant them. Their denseness makes them easy to use as topiaries, but they also do well when shaped around a metal or wooden frame.

If you will freehand your boxwood topiary — that is, without a frame — your best shape choices include either a cone or a ball. If your desired shape is more complex, then a frame is strongly recommended.

You need to prune boxwoods several times a year. Use long-handled shears to make shaping and cutting easier without straining your wrists. Prune every three months, cutting away longer growths that shoot out beyond your desired shape. Never prune more than 3 inches. As you prune, your boxwood will become bushier. If you live in a cold climate, choose a rounded shape on the top so heavy snow and ice will not damage the boxwood.

If you are using a frame, choose a form that will fit around the shape of your boxwood. Take the frame apart at its center seam, and then place the two sides of the frame on either side of your boxwood, and push any rods into the soil around the boxwood. Next, pull the branches of your boxwood through the frame, and then begin to cut a rough shape of your topiary. Over time, your topiary will take on its intended form.

English yew

The **English yew**, the oldest tree in Europe, is another popular choice as a topiary because it grows low — about 2 to 4 feet high and 10 feet wide — and responds well to heavy pruning. They also can thrive in the shade, although they do just as well in full sunlight. When selecting a yew plant, ask about its growth pattern because yews come in a variety of shapes. The growth pattern should correspond to the shape of the topiary you want to create.

While most topiaries are best grown from young plants, yew topiaries can do well when shaped from an old, overgrown plant because yews are dense and stems sprout vigorously, even from old wood. Another reason to use an already established yew for your topiary is because yews grow slowly.

Yews are extremely hardy and can handle periods of drought. Prune your yew at least once a year but preferably twice a year after new shoots appear, in late spring and mid-autumn.

Hollies

Hollies are evergreens suited to trimming. They require full to partial sun and do well in freezing temperatures. In fact, holly is one of the most prunable plants, but make sure you wear gloves to protect against its spiky leaves. When dealing with hollies, remember you need to properly drain them, you should not water them too much, and you should not disturb the roots; transplanting a holly would probably harm the plant. They do bounce back if they drop their leaves, growing new ones quickly. Hollies come in a variety of types and sizes, making these plants a great choice when creating topiaries. But, they also grow slowly so if you plan to create a large topiary, choose one close to the size you need your sculpture.

Juniper

Junipers are popular evergreen plants and are used as topiaries because their narrow, needled leaves are easily shaped. The plant also withstands more severe pruning than many other plants. They are also popular because they do well in both cold/dry and hot/dry climates, and they can survive in just about any type of soil. Most junipers grow slowly, although some varieties grow quickly, which means they need little pruning — about once a year — so they will keep their topiary shape longer. Slow growth also means you will need to choose a mature juniper close in size to your desired sculpture.

Traditional juniper topiaries include ball and pad styles, or round and square shapes, but junipers are suitable for whatever shape you choose to create. Use hand shears and create your shape, pruning away any unnecessary branches. If you decide to create balls, cones, and spirals, garden wire may help and lessen the chances of snipping too much. Junipers mostly grow slowly so if you overdo your pruning, you will have to wait until the next year to correct your mistakes.

Once you have shaped your juniper, ignore any new shoots emerging in the early spring. Wait until mid-June to prune any of the stems. If you prune a Juniper too soon in spring, you could bruise the sappy new growth and damage the shape of your topiary. By mid-June, the juniper's leaves will be stronger and can withstand pruning. If you do need to prune again, wait until September. But, always remove dead branches because they are susceptible to disease.

Although, as stated, most junipers are slow growers, there are a few fast-growing junipers, such as the Pfitzer juniper. This variety can grow 12 to 18 inches per year. Because of the speed of growth, these junipers may need trimming two or three times a year. In this case, trim back new growths, even if they are inside the plant. Do not be afraid to prune some parts back to the previous year's wood in order to keep your topiary shape and size.

Arborvitae

The **arborvitae** is a cold-weather evergreen in the cypress family. It is popular because, beyond needing moist, alkaline soil and cool temperatures, it does not need much care. It has a natural cone shape and dense foliage that makes it a favorite choice as a topiary, particularly if you seek a spiral shape.

Arborvitae grows fast and reaches heights of more than 40 feet. Their popular, soft, fan-like leaves and beauty make them a favorite in many gardens. You can plant them in full sun or partial shade and maintain them easily, but you must protect them with netting if you live in a cold climate — snow and ice can damage their soft branches. Arborvitaes only need pruning once a year, but you should do it in fall or early winter. If you prune arborvitaes in spring or summer, their tips will turn brown.

Use pruning shears for your arborvitae topiary, and go slowly, especially if you hope to achieve a smooth, spiral shape. An easy way to prune this shape is to tie a ribbon to the top tip of the tree. Wind the ribbon around the plant, starting at the top of the tree working all the way down to the base. Wind the ribbon at the width you want your spiral. Start your pruning halfway down the tree and prune up. Remove one-third of each branch above the ribbon, but stop when you have reached 1 foot from the top of the tree. Step back every now and then to make sure you prune on track. Next, move downward, again cutting one-third of the branches above the ribbon, until you reach the bottom of the plant. The bottom half's pattern should match the top half's. When you finish that, go back to the top of the tree, and cut each branch you want to remove to about a ½ inch from the trunk. Do not cut the branches that are part of your spiral, only the larger ones. Now, step back, and take a look at your topiary. Remove any uneven branches until you have your desired spiral shape. Once you have done this, you should only need to prune your arborvitae topiary once a year.

Bonsai

If you are looking for an artistic challenge in pruning styles, you might want to try your shears at creating a **bonsai**. It is not a particular plant, as some people think, but rather a Japanese word used to describe the growing of plants in shallow trays or pots, particularly woody plants. Bonsai is a miniature version of a tree planted in a pot or tray.

Although the history of bonsai was not well documented, bonsai existed as an artistic form in China about 2,000 years ago. By the 1100s, the plant art form spread to Japan and began to gain popularity. The Japanese perfected the art of bonsai, and it became an important part of their culture. The idea behind the technique of bonsai is that the plant you choose, the pruning you do, and the mood you create are choices decided by and unique to you. You choose every aspect of your plant, from the container to the shape of the branches. Constant pruning keeps the bonsai small and healthy and prevents it from potentially growing into a huge tree or bushy shrub. Perhaps one of the most interesting traits about bonsai is that you never finish creating it. When you choose this artistic form of pruning, you are in it for the long haul.

If you are creating a traditional bonsai, choose a dwarf or a slow-growing plant. Your plant should range in height from 3 inches to 3 feet. You can choose either an evergreen tree or a deciduous one, but make sure it has either short needles or small leaves because trees with smaller needles or leaves will look in better proportion to the small bonsai you are about to create.

Also, choose a plant that does not mind poor, rocky soil. Moist soil rich in nutrients will cause your tree to grow quickly and fuller, which will create a more difficult job for you, especially if you have never done a bonsai before. If your tree's shape is distorted or stunted, this simply adds to your design. In the world of bonsai, a tree with growth predominantly on one side or thick at the base of the trunk is particularly favored. You can purchase plants and tools for bonsai online from websites like Sleepy Hollow Bonsai (**www.shbonsai.com/index.html**).

Once you have picked out your bonsai plant and your container — either a shallow tray or pot — start with the roots and untangle them, cutting off any too long to fit in your container. If you are growing your tree in a shallow tray and it has a taproot in addition to feeder roots, cut off the taproot. Then, carefully replant your tree in your container with fresh soil.

Now, you are ready to do some initial pruning. This means making a decision on how you want your bonsai to grow and having a mental picture in your mind on how you want it to look when finished. If you have no idea, look at photographs of bonsai plants, or visit the Bonsai Site's gallery of pictures (**www.bonsaisite.com**).

To start your pruning, clip off some of the branches to thin out your plant. Your goal is to make the tree look old because that is the premise of the bonsai look. Prune these branches close to the trunk. Next, prune back the top so your tree is less than 4 feet tall but at least 3 inches tall, according to the shape and size you desire. Shorten the trunk to a few inches above the desired height. Heavily water your tree, and then cover it and its pot with a clear plastic bag. Place your tree in a cool place where it will receive light but not direct sunlight, and leave it this way for two to three weeks while it recovers from the pruning. Then, place it in direct sunlight.

There are two schools of thought when it comes to training your tree to grow into a bonsai shape. Some growers prefer training their plant immediately after planting it in its container; others like to wait several weeks to a year in order for the plant to get established in its container. You should consider the characteristics of your chosen plant type when you decide. Before you begin to train the shape of your bonsai, make sure you consider the time of year and the type of plant you are using:

- If you choose an evergreen bonsai, train it in fall or winter before its new growth for the year begins.

- If your bonsai is a deciduous tree, train it in early summer when its sap is flowing, and it is more flexible.

- Do not train your bonsai in the spring because you can damage its tender, dormant buds.

- You can use wire to force your tree to keep its desired shape. Before you can use the wire, the buds need to be growing so that the wire placed around them in training will not damage them.

- When dealing with a plant with a heavy trunk, you will need 8- to 9-gauge aluminum or copper wire.

- When training a plant with a smaller trunk or when shaping the branches and tops of larger trees, use 18- or 20-gauge aluminum or copper wire.

Once you have decided when to train your plant and which wire to use, stick the wire through the holes in the bottom of your pot or container, and wrap it around your plant upward in a 45-degree spiral. Carefully bend your tree to the desired shape. The wire will hold it in place. Slip little pieces of paper under the wire as you bend the trunk. This will protect the bark. You can remove the wire once your tree grows in its new shape; for deciduous trees, this will occur after three or four months, but evergreens may take as long as a year. Do not leave the wire on any longer than necessary, or you run the risk of your tree growing around it, which will permanently disfigure the trunk.

Keep a close eye on your bonsai to make sure it is growing according to plan. Pinch off any sprouts growing in the wrong places, and prune branches growing too long. Decide which side of your bonsai is the front. This will be the side you want to look old and thinned out. In the back, allow the foliage to grow denser. This will give your tree body and will also produce additional leaves for healthy growth. Also, allow one branch near the bottom of your tree to grow freely. This free-growing limb will use most of your tree's energy so it is easier to shape the remainder of the plant. Once your tree is trained, clip off this branch, and seal or paint the wound.

After a few years, you will need to revisit your bonsai's root system, as your tree will become **root bound,** meaning the roots will tangle together from growing in a contained space. If your bonsai is a deciduous tree, you will need to re-pot it every year or two. If it is an evergreen, you will have to re-pot it every two to four years, depending on the age of the tree. Carefully tip the tree out of its pot; if the roots have become a thick, tight ball, it is time to re-pot. Wash off the soil by gently swishing the roots in water. Next, cut off a third of the roots growing on the outside of the root ball. Also, prune off part of the large, fleshy roots, but make sure they are not attached to the large, fibrous roots. Then replant your tree in the same pot, using fresh soil. Water it, and cover it with a clear plastic bag, and again, keep it in a cool place out of direct sunlight for two to three weeks.

Bonsai-style pruning in the garden

Although a true bonsai tree is grown in a shallow tray or container, you can also create the style and influence in your garden. The look is best achieved with trees growing on uneven land. The idea is to create a small tree that resembles an older, larger tree. Any tree can be dwarfed in this manner, but the best choices are slow-growing conifers and dwarf trees or shrubs.

Start by pruning some of the branches at the trunk of your tree, especially any long or large limbs. Train the remaining branches by wrapping aluminum or copper wire around them in a 45-degree spiral. First, stick the base of the wire in the ground, bend the tree carefully, and spiral the wire upward. After your tree has had a season of growth, you can remove the wire. During its growing season, pinch and snip new sprouts, and do your heavy pruning when your tree is dormant in late fall. You may also have to do occasional root pruning.

Choosing your bonsai

Technically, you can grow and prune any plant as a bonsai. But some trees make particularly good choices in the art of creating a bonsai. Sometimes people confuse bonsai with dwarfing a tree, but the latter involves permanently creating genetic miniatures of trees, whereas a bonsai is a plant that looks like a miniature tree because of training, pruning, root reduction, defoliation, and grafting. A dwarf tree may need occasional pruning, as all trees do, but a bonsai is a lifelong effort.

Juniper

Juniper, a woody, poplar evergreen, makes a great choice when creating a bonsai because it can handle severe pruning, and it is easy for even a beginner to create the perfect bonsai look of an aged tree. Because it is an evergreen, it will need its roots pruned in early spring or late fall. Junipers need full sunlight occasionally so if your juniper bonsai is an inside bonsai, you should place it where it will receive morning sunlight — at least two hours a day — with afternoon shade.

When growing your juniper bonsai, you need to pinch off any new growth as soon as it appears. If you do not, then branches will form, and your juniper will appear ragged instead of aged — the look of a true bonsai. If your juniper is an inside bonsai, you will also need to prune its roots every other spring by removing it from its tray or pot. Prune off one-third of the roots, and then re-plant it in the container with two-thirds-part fresh soil and one-thrid-part sand. Mist your juniper's leaves twice a day for two weeks. This will help your tree get over the shock that can result from pruning its roots and then re-planting.

Although junipers are considered hassle-free trees, you should not become inattentive when taking care of your juniper bonsai. A juniper can appear healthy even if it has died. This picture of health can appear for weeks or even months after the tree has stopped growing. In addition, junipers need seasonal variations in temperature so if your juniper bonsai is an indoor plant, you must place it outside from time to time. But, do not place your tree outside during extremely cold or hot times because juniper does not like extreme temperatures.

Chinese elm

Chinese elms are a popular choice for creating bonsai because they are strong, sturdy, and handle extensive pruning without going into shock. This tree adapts to various climates and does well both indoors or outdoors.

Chinese elms benefit from having all of their small, serrated leaves pruned off just after the leaves have expanded. This forces a second group of leaves to sprout that tend to be smaller and more in line with the small size of a bonsai tree. Chinese elms grow fast, and you can leaf prune twice in the spring and again in the fall, when the color of second group of leaves tend to be more vibrant.

If your tree needs major branch pruning, do it in late spring or early summer, when the tree is at its strongest, but be careful not to prune too much because you could weaken your tree. A good rule of thumb is to simply go on your feelings, and prune your Chinese elm when it looks like it needs pruning. Remove sucker growths at the base of the plant.

Chinese elms are versatile when it comes to creating bonsai. You can either prune off the branches to get your desired form, or you can use the wiring method. When working with wire, wrap it around the top and the side branches you want to grow, while pruning off unnecessary branches on the opposite side of the tree. Make sure you circle the wire at a 45-degree angle, and do not wrap it too tightly because the wire could scar the bark. The bare side missing branches becomes the front of your Chinese elm, and the wired side becomes the back. Take care to keep tabs on your tree if you choose the wiring approach: Chinese elms grow fast so your wiring could wind up embedding into the tree if left unattended. After the tree's branches are growing in the desired direction, you can remove the wire.

Your best time to root prune is in spring when your tree's leaves begin to bud. The Chinese elm can handle extensive

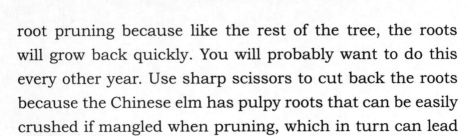

root pruning because like the rest of the tree, the roots will grow back quickly. You will probably want to do this every other year. Use sharp scissors to cut back the roots because the Chinese elm has pulpy roots that can be easily crushed if mangled when pruning, which in turn can lead to root rot.

You can plant Chinese elms as outdoor bonsais because they can handle varying temperatures, including as low as 20 degrees in winter. You will need to protect its roots in cold temperatures by putting mulch or insulating material around the base of the tree. Thanks to its stocky build and quick growth pattern, you can easily prune any bonsai style you desire. As with a bonsai grown in a container, you should cut off new growth immediately or use a wire until you have trained your Chinese elm to grow in the pattern you have chosen.

A Chinese elm bonsai grown in the ground will need to have its roots pruned, just like a bonsai in a container, in order to maintain its small stature. The best time to do this is in the late fall and early spring. Push your shovel into the ground in a circle around your Chinese elm, about 2 to 4 feet from the trunk. Chinese elms are also prone to surface roots. You can do little about surface roots because cutting them off can kill a tree. But, keep in mind that a rocky, unlevel ground surface in a garden is the perfect visual setting for a bonsai.

Myrtle

Myrtles are naturally dense plants that are easily pruned to create bonsai. This tree tolerates some shade but must also have plenty of sunlight, and its container must provide good drainage. It makes an excellent choice as a bonsai because the dry air of central heating or air conditioning do not bother it, and it adapts to household atmospheric conditions. While myrtles are a huge family of plants, the crape myrtle, in its many varieties, is normally used as a bonsai plant because of its beautiful flowers and attractive red and silver peeling bark.

Crape myrtles are native to Japan and Korea, but today they are found throughout the United States and all over the world. Crape myrtles are known as low-maintenance plants, but when creating a bonsai, there is always maintenance needed to keep it small over its lifespan and in the form of the bonsai. They are deciduous plants, and their large variety of colors make them a popular choice for bonsai, particularly because they are hardy and can tolerate the extensive pruning involved.

Most crape myrtles used for creating bonsais are of the dwarf variety. Whether indoors or out, they need a sunny area and good drainage. Because crape myrtles are favored for their beautiful flowers that bloom on the short shoots of the current year's growth, you will need to be extremely careful with how you prune your bonsai to ensure your plant flowers again the following year. Prune your heavier branches in the fall when your tree has no flowers. This will stimulate bud production for the following year, and heavy pruning will thicken the trunk. In the spring, let new shoots grow for several weeks, until you are into late spring or early summer. At that time, cut back new shoots to two or three leaves so the buds at the **axils** of these leaves, or the point where the leaf attaches to the stem, will produce new flower-bearing shoots.

When creating your bonsai shape, wire the trunk and branches from the spring to the fall. Be careful of how tight you wind the wire on the crape myrtle's smooth bark to prevent any scarring or damage. The crape myrtle's delicate branches make it easy to train so you can also forgo the wiring if you desire a bonsai with a broom look. In the year after you train your plant, pinch off any new growths. This will promote branch ramification, which will give your crape myrtle bonsai the desired look of a large tree in a smaller form.

Pine

Pines are a classic favorite of bonsai fans, yet they are also one of the most difficult choices. Unlike deciduous trees and many conifers — which produce new leaves on a continuous basis — pines only have one growth spurt each year, or sometimes two growth spurts if the pines grow in mild climate. In addition, it is time consuming to train a pine to the perfect bonsai shape. But once that shape is reached, pines are easier to maintain than other bonsai plants because they require little routine maintenance.

By shortening the candles, which is the new growth, or expanding new growth shoots, which are what the candles become as the needles lengthen and cluster from a single stem, you can control the size of a bonsai pine. Expanding new growth shoots simply means that you pinch back the new shoots. This will keep your pine from growing larger and will make your bonsai fuller and bushier. You should remember that although they only have one or two growth spurts each year, their growth spurt is extensive, making them fast growers so choosing a pine for your bonsai creation means you must be willing to give it the time and attention it will demand. The best time to do your pruning is in late spring so your pine does not lose too much sap.

Use wiring when creating your pine bonsai. Wiring trains your tree's branches and trunk to grow in the direction you desire, and it also slows the flow of its sap and helps to distribute energy and vigor throughout your pine instead of just directing the energy to the branch tips. A popular pine bonsai shape is one with a completely straight, upright, and tapered trunk, although the idea behind the bonsai is that your tree can be any shape you choose. To create this popular shape, prune off the bottom branches, and position the first main branch of your bonsai about one-third of the way up the trunk. The rest of the branches should spiral upward above this main branch, growing tighter as they reach the **apex** or top of the tree, thus forming the shape of a triangle.

Spruce

Spruce is another evergreen you can create into a bonsai but can prove to be a frustrating choice, especially if you are new to the bonsai game. Spruces are difficult to train, especially through wiring. They are also difficult to style. The time commitment for this tree may be greater, but it does not mean you should avoid choosing a spruce as your bonsai. If you do not feel experienced enough, you can always try your hand at another type of tree first in order to get a feel for what is involved in this type of artistic pruning.

There are 35 varieties of spruce in the United States alone, including some dwarf species. When purchasing a spruce, do not buy a variety that is grafted because they tend to bulge at the base. You can tell if your spruce has been grafted by the color of its needles. Green spruces have color variations that range from green to blue, whereas blue spruces are entirely blue and almost all have been produced from grafting. If you do not know for sure if a spruce has been grafted, ask the nursery you are purchasing it from.

When creating your bonsai, prune back the tree's side branches and its visible dormant buds. In the spring, the lateral shoots will appear. When the shoots are about 1 inch long, pinch them to make your spruce bonsai denser.

Leave any major pruning until late summer or fall because spruces are sensitive trees and will not tolerate pruning in spring when they grow the most.

During the fall or winter, when the tree does not grow as quickly and tolerates it better, you can wire the branches for training. Spruces have thick branches so use thick wiring when training your spruce as you desire. Also, use the wiring to bend those branches at least 1 inch thick so you do not risk breaking or snapping a limb. Otherwise, the branches may die back quickly. Because of the natural pyramid-shaped growth pattern of spruce, you might want to consider pruning this shape when creating your bonsai.

Compared to other bonsai plant types, spruce bonsais need a larger root ball so your container may be deeper than a traditional bonsai tray or pot. When you do prune the roots, cut them by one-third, and plant them in fast-draining soil. Do not start wiring or branch pruning until the plant has been in the container for three months after you pruned its roots.

CASE STUDY: TALKING WITH A BONSAI EXPERT

Ashley Carrier is a principal bonsai expert at Bonsai Outlet. See www.bonsaioutlet.com.

When considering why and in what ways to prune your bonsai, remember two guiding principles:

- You are emulating a full-growth tree.

- You are encouraging the health and aesthetic of your miniaturized bonsai tree.

In addition, ask yourself whether you are pruning to form your bonsai or to maintain your bonsai once you established the form. Form pruning lays the foundation for maintenance pruning and is more drastic and takes a longer time from which to recuperate than maintenance pruning.

Pruning your bonsai at the appropriate time depends upon the species of your tree. Your best time, though, is when your tree produces new growth. For deciduous trees — maple and cherry — early spring is your better choice. Pines and spruces fair better in mid-spring, while early to midsummer is recommended for junipers.

Learn your bonsai cycles, and time your pruning accordingly. With deciduous trees, pinch back new shoots to two pairs of leaves, while removing any shoots growing vertically. Pines should have their candles reduced by approximately one-half, with the ones remaining being shortened. You pinch back the new shoots on spruces to half their length to encourage buds to form at the base rather than at the growing end. Because junipers push out new growth throughout their growing season, you should thin that growth regularly to avoid overgrowth that causes self-shading.

You should perform all pruning with clean hands and sharp scissors, pruning shears, or leaf trimmers. For example, leaf pruning — defoliation — to reduce the leaf size or to get rid of unattractive leaves is done by cutting approximately two-thirds of the leaves from your bonsai tree directly behind the leaf. The quality and condition of your tools can significantly affect the appearance and health of your bonsai.

Chapter 8

Pruning Deciduous Trees

Deciduous plants drop all of their leaves in fall or winter. Deciduous trees are divided into four groups determined by their leaf type, as well as leaf arrangement. These include:

1. Simple leaves located opposite each other on the stem. Maples and tree lilacs are examples of opposite simple leaf trees.

2. Simple leaves located alternately on the stem. Birch, poplars, and willows are alternate simple leaf trees.

3. Compound leaves located opposite each other on the stem. Ash and buckeye are examples of opposite compound leaf trees.

4. Compound leaves located alternately on the stem. Locust and walnut are examples of alternate compound leaf trees.

Deciduous leaves also come in four types: smooth, finely toothed, double-toothed sharp pointed, and lobed.

Some common types of deciduous trees include maple, crabapple, magnolia, and cottonwood. You should primarily prune these plants to create a strong, well-balanced branch system that, in turn, makes the plant more attractive and healthier. Aside from these reasons, you need to prune a deciduous tree in cases of storm damage from heavy snows or high winds or when a tree's growth interferes with utility wires, poles, pathways, or buildings.

You also want to prune to remove dead or diseased branches because these could cause injury or property damage. In this case, you prune for safety reasons and for the health of the tree. Health also comes into play when you prune the crown of a tree to increase airflow and also reduce some pests. Storm damage can leave a ragged wound in the tree. A severe wound may not seal and can kill the tree. Pruning a damaged tree helps the tree heal and, thus, produces a healthier tree.

Pruning Young Trees

You should not prune young trees until the second year after you plant them because leaves provide a young tree or shrub with nourishment needed when first planted in the ground, and the buds on the ends of the branches send hormones to the roots that promote growth. Once you begin to prune, do it carefully and gradually because removing too many branches will slow the growth of the tree.

Do not rush when cutting off branches; rather, you should prune gradually, especially if you are new at the technique. Plan which branches you want to prune before you begin. Pruning should make the plant look better and keep it healthy, and random cuts will leave you with an ugly, unhealthy tree. Unless you are creating a specialized shape — as in the cases of bonsai, topiary, pleaching, or standards — keep to your tree's natural shape.

Begin by cutting just above an outward-facing bud. In spring, this bud will produce a side shoot that grows away from the tree. Do not prune any of the pink-colored growths because these are new growths from the previous year. Prune any black-colored shoots, and make sure you prune these by the third year. By the tree's fifth year, it is considered a mature tree. From this point on, prune all growth from the center of the tree and also any dead or diseased branches.

If you want to create a **landscaped tree**, or a tree that has been arranged or pruned in order to provide a desired visual picture, you would want to have a length of bare trunk with a crown at the top. A bare trunk gives the tree some clearance room underneath. You can prune back the central leader branch so you get a bushier tree, but you have to spend a good deal of time pruning the tree every year, as another branch will try to take over as the leader. When pruning deciduous trees, leave the trunk and leader branch alone, and instead prune off branches that form narrow angles with the trunk. Also, prune branches that crowd the interior of the plant or do not flow with the shape you are creating. In addition, you will need to prune the suckers that grow from the base, as well as water sprouts growing upright from the branches.

Light pruning — only removing small, damaged, or diseased branches — can be done at any time of the year. You must do it sparingly so your tree does not bleed. For more extensive pruning, the most favorable time to prune deciduous trees is late winter to early spring when the tree is dormant. Winter is also when fewer insects can feed on the wound and cause damage to the tree's health. The exceptions to these standard pruning rules are birches and maples. These trees will bleed sap in spring, and you should prune them in the coldest part of winter when they are fully dormant. This allows ample time for wound closure to occur in late summer to early fall when maples will lose less sap.

If your tree produces blooms on new wood, usually in summer, prune in late winter or early spring. When a tree is pruned before new growth appears, it will produce more flowers. If your tree blooms on old wood, usually in spring, do your pruning immediately after the blooms fade so you can avoid cutting off new flower buds. This will stimulate growth of more buds for the following year. You should understand the important characteristics of your tree before you prune it. Be sure to confirm its type when you purchase the tree or before you start to prune.

Finally, pruning at the correct time of year negates the necessity of having to dress or paint the wound, even though that is often discouraged. It was once believed that dressing or pruning paint was essential to seal the wound, but this is no longer the school of thought. In fact, dressing or pruning paint can actually harbor microorganisms and also slow the tree's ability to heal its wounds.

Ornamental Pruning

Ornamental deciduous trees — typically smaller trees than the other trees in your garden — produce colorful flowers or leaves, instantly adding a focal point to your yard. Most ornamental trees average about 25 feet in height and include crabapple, dogwood, cherry, plum, pear, red bud, and magnolia.

Just as with all deciduous trees, the reasons for pruning remain the same: health, beauty, and safety. First, remove any dead or diseased branches, which you can do any time of year. If the limb is small, use pruning shears. For larger branches, use a pruning saw.

For more extensive pruning, prune during the tree's dormancy period, usually during winter or early spring. Start from the bottom of the tree, and prune upward. Prune branches at the collar, cut at an angle, and leave a small part of that collar on the trunk. Remove lower limbs because they can weaken the tree. Once you have removed those lower branches in accordance with the overall shape you seek, prune limbs and water sprouts from the inside of the tree to the outside. Make sure to remove all water sprouts because these can easily overtake your tree. Also, make sure you keep your tree trunk as a single stem so it grows strong and less likely breaks in extreme weather conditions. Prune any cross branches. If your ornamental tree is by a sidewalk or lines your driveway, also prune any branches that may obstruct vision or make it difficult for pedestrians to pass on the sidewalk. As always, prune with purpose, but also prune gradually. Do not be afraid to step back and observe your handiwork to ensure thoughtful and creative pruning.

This well-pruned deciduous tree is an ornamental addition to a garden in Florida.

Chapter 9:

Pruning Popular Fruit Trees

The goal, when it comes to fruit trees, is to prune them so they produce the most fruit as possible. This usually involves cutting off the lower branches in order to direct more energy, light, and air to the top of the tree. This will, in turn, enable the tree to produce more fruit and will prevent heavy fruit from weighing down and damaging the lower parts of the tree. You should learn about a specific fruit tree's natural growth habits and shape, as well as the age of the tree, before undertaking any pruning. Remember, different species of fruit trees require different pruning methods. Only prune as much as necessary in order to create the desired shape of the tree while also allowing light and air to reach the center of the tree. If removing branches, cut just below the collar, but if pruning branches back, cut above the outward-facing bud.

Also, pay attention to the age of your tree. If your fruit tree is young, your goal is to train it and help the tree develop branches strong enough to support its crop. If the tree is a single stem, remove shoots as it grows its side branches. If your young fruit tree has branches, keep the ones that are wide angled and in a good position, and prune those that are not. Also, prune branches growing too close to your desired branches. But, do not prune a young tree more than necessary — less is best — or you will delay fruiting. Keep in mind, though, you want to wait until your tree is 2 years old before allowing it to bear fruit. Bearing fruit before then will weaken your tree, and this will delay the production of more fruit for several years. With a mature fruit tree, perform annual pruning to reduce the fruit load and stimulate new shoot growth. To do this, prune branches to keep the fruit tree's desired size and shape, pinch off excess flowers, and rid the tree of dead or diseased wood or branches that cross or rub on each other. Pinching excess flowers will help keep the tree's fruit production steady. Pay particular attention to each type of fruit tree's specific pruning needs.

Peach Trees

Peach trees, fruit trees that produce heavy loads, are often considered a challenge to grow because these trees are sensitive to soil type, climate, and cold. These challenges have not prevented people living in northern climates from attempting to grow peach trees.

The peach tree originated in China and then made its way to Turkey and Persia (Iran) via trade routes, eventually ending up in Europe. From there, the French brought it to America in the 1500s. Peach trees make an attractive addition to any garden because of their beautiful, dark green leaves and pink flowers, not to mention their delectable fruit. This tree is related to the almond tree, needs pruning on a regular basis because it grows fast, and can average 6 to 10 feet high. If you do not prune on a regular basis, you could shorten the tree's lifespan or expose it to disease, particularly a disease called leaf curl. **Leaf curl** is a fungus that harms the leaves of a peach tree, which, in turn, affects the amount of fruit the tree will bear. Pruning annually helps guarantee that your peach tree will bear fruit. Also, peach trees tend to become overgrown on the lower limbs so annual pruning will keep this in check.

With young peach trees, you should prune carefully so the wood that produces fruit remains near the center of the tree. The farther away from the center of the tree a branch grows, the poorer the quality of fruit and the less fruit the tree produces. For young trees, summer is a favorable time to prune in order to develop the desired tree frame. This also lessens the dormant pruning needed during its first winter when young trees are more susceptible to winter injuries and borer infestation. Pruning in the summer also allow you to encourage a spreading growth method of branches that extend outward and upward.

The best time to prune your mature peach tree, if you want to encourage more fruit bearing, is in the late winter or early spring, when small pink buds begin to form. Do not prune later than the end of February because peach trees can start to bloom in early March. Next, remove water sprouts and any branches that are not fruit bearing. This is important because on peach trees, water sprouts can get quite hardy and will prevent light from reaching the lower branches. As a result, fruit will grow higher on the tree, out of picking reach. In addition, peach trees are susceptible to disease. Pruning at this time will allow wounds to heal quicker, when growth begins.

Use large pruning shears, and prune those branches pointing upward while leaving those growing at a 90-degree angle from the trunk of the tree. With peach trees, you also want to prune in one of two methods: the modified leader or open center. The **modified leader** is easier to maintain because a peach tree grows with a central leader, and in this method, the central trunk is allowed to branch off to form several tops. You will need to cut back the top annually to shorten your tree and also to allow more light to hit the lower branches. Also, prune any cross branches, especially those near the trunk of the tree. Pruning off cross branches will improve airflow throughout your tree and will also allow more sunlight to reach fruit-producing branches. If any branches break off — which can happen on weaker branches producing fruit — cut them off past the breaking point, where the twig meets the branch. Aim to prune about 40 percent of the tree, but do not overdo your pruning. Although 40 percent sounds high, you will create a more attractive tree and a healthier one as well.

In the **open center** method, also known as the vase method, and the most popular choice for pruning peach trees, you produce a tree that has a weaker branch structure but allows for easier access to fruit. Peaches are a lightweight fruit and are considered a good choice for this type of pruning. If the open center method is your choice, you prune so the limbs form a vase effect and are not all growing out of the main trunk close to each other; otherwise, they will form a cluster of weak crotches. The whole center remains open, but you will need to thin the branches and remove older branches. This method allows for more light to reach the shady interior of the tree.

You also need to thin out the fruit from time to time. Peach trees produce large fruit and only bear fruit on 1-year-old stems. By pruning to keep the branch system open, you can yield more fruit. Fruit should be about 6 inches apart because each peach needs about 35 leaves to nourish it. Also prune any drooping stems and short stems because these tend to produce smaller peaches. A well-pruned peach tree has branches with enough spacing to allow a bird to fly through its crown.

Pruning peach trees can be labor intensive, since, as mentioned, they grow vigorously. But, if you are willing to make the effort, the payoff is a steady crop of tasty fruit.

Apple Trees

The apple tree is a favorite fruit tree because there are so many different varieties to choose from, including those you can create yourself, as apple trees take well to grafting. Apple trees originated in Europe, but you can now find them in North America, the United Kingdom, Europe, and Asia. There are 7,500 varieties worldwide, with 2,500 varieties in the United States, including the most familiar: Red Delicious, Granny Smith, Golden Delicious, Gala, Pink Lady, Fuji, and Crabapple. They prefer moist soil and need cold winters in order for the seeds to sprout, which is why you rarely find apple trees in dry or extremely hot climates. In North America, apple trees grow best in Zones 3 through 8. They also need full sun and extensive pruning, and you will need to spray or find a natural way to control the many insects and diseases that can plague the apple tree.

Apple trees, like most fruit trees, are medium-sized trees. When left to grow naturally, an apple tree can grow to about 15 to 20 feet, with some varieties reaching up to 40 feet. The trunk tends to be short, with branches extending out not far from the ground. Like most flowering fruit trees, apple trees are part of the large rose family. The tree flowers in the spring through the summer, with the fruit ripening in the fall. The apple tree's fragrant flowers, delicious fruit, and visual attractiveness, even when bare in winter, often make this fruit tree a centerpiece in many gardens.

Because apple trees take well to grafting, they tolerate different types of pruning so you can tailor your pruning to your own specific needs and desires. When choosing your pruning method, keep two goals in mind: If your tree is young, you want to create a strong, sturdy tree able to withstand the elements and disease; and if your tree is a mature apple tree, you want to prune so it maintains its shape and can produce the best and most fruit as possible.

This gardener uses shears to prune an apple tree in March.

A young apple tree's first few years will have a large impact on how it produces fruit later on in its life. If you are planting a young apple tree, it will either be a whip or single stem or perhaps more developed as a feathered tree — that is, already having side branches. Choosing a whip or feathered tree may depend on your finances, since the latter is more expensive. Nurseries sell most apple trees bare root. Before planting it into the ground, observe the roots closely. Tease out the roots on the outside of the root ball with a stick or a fork in order to encourage them to grow into the surrounding soil. If you cannot tease out these roots because they have grown too tightly around each other, make some vertical slits in the root ball with a knife until you can pull out some roots. You do not want the roots to fold so if your hole is not wide enough or you do not want to dig it wide enough to accommodate them, cut them back so they fit easily into the hole. Then, cover them with the soil you dug out as you proceed to plant your tree.

During the first years after planting, the tree will lay down its permanent framework of branches so you want to help it develop branches strong enough to bear fruit. If you want to yield a crop of large apples, then you will want to pinch off flower buds so less energy is drawn from the tree. This results in fewer areas in which the plant has to distribute food so you wind up with larger flowers and, thus, larger fruit.

Other fruit trees produce fruit on either limbs or spurs, which are short, stubby branches that grow in between limbs. But apple trees are unique because their fruit can grow on both limbs and spurs, depending on the variety of tree. If your apple tree produces fruit on spurs, you will need to prune some of the fruit in order to encourage the tree to produce bigger and better fruit on the remainder of the spurs. An apple tree's spurs will produce fruit for several years, but once it has stopped producing fruit on that particular spur, you will need to cut it off so your tree can grow a replacement. You will know when to do this by the appearance of the spur — it starts looking aged.

Begin your pruning in late winter or early spring. You do not want to prune when there is new growth later in the spring or in the summer because the tree will bleed too much sap, unless you are removing suckers or water sprouts. You can also remove any branches broken by winter storms or that may have died from the cold during the spring. Other than that, you only want to prune during the apple tree's dormant period. Bare branches also make it easier for you to see which branches need pruning and which do not.

There are three forms of pruning used when pruning an apple tree: the central leader, the open center, and the modified central leader. If you are growing your tree to have a central leader, then you want a single, dominant leader in the center of the tree, with branches growing off it that decrease in length as they move up to the top of the tree. These branches are called scaffold branches or main branches. If you chose an open center form, your tree will have a vase shape, with three or four leaders growing outward and upward from the trunk. Branches will grow off these leaders. If you choose a modified central leader, you will have a combination of the central leader and open center forms. In this pruning form, you allow a central leader to grow until the tree reaches about 7 feet. Then, you bend the leader over to a weak side branch to stop its growth. Your choice of form often depends on the natural growth of your apple tree.

Many nurseries sell apples trees as three-in-one or five-in-one types of apple varieties, the result of three or more types of apple trees grafted together. If you purchase this type of apple tree, you will want to prune your tree to have an open center, which will allow more light to reach the interior of the tree. Once you have selected three or four side branches, you will need to cut the central stem off at a point just above the highest side branch. This will allow your tree to continue to grow upward and outward from the side branches.

If you have chosen the central leader form, you will need to select the side branches you want to remain with care because it will determine the future shape of your tree, as well as the tree's strength. Allow each side branch to have enough space to develop. Begin by leaving one branch about 2 feet from the ground, with the remaining branches about 6 inches to 18 inches apart as you move up the trunk. Try to keep your branches in a spiral arrangement. This will allow each branch to have enough room to grow, and it will also prevent each branch from being robbed of minerals and water coming up from the roots of another branch.

During the first few years of growth, your tree may look sparse, and you may feel tempted to keep branches closer together or closer to the ground. Remember, the location of these branches will never change throughout the life of the tree so if you leave too many on the tree, they will thicken and grow too close together as the tree ages.

If you have chosen a modified central leader as your form for your apple tree, make sure you still have a dominant, strong central leader. If you have two strong leaders, you will need to remove one completely and immediately.

If you do not have room for the average-sized apple tree, consider a dwarf or semi-dwarf, which average 5 to 12 feet in height. Often, dwarf fruit trees are less hardy than trees of average height, can easily break in high winds or heavy snows, and are more susceptible to insect infestation and disease. Dwarfing an apple tree yourself is a better alternative. To do this, you will need to cut a strip of bark about a ¾ inch wide completely around the tree during the early summer. When you do this, make sure you make the cut close to the bark but not in the wood. Do this carefully because a sharp cut into the tree can kill it. After you remove the bark, turn it upside down, and put it back around the tree so the green side faces inward. Then, cover the repair with grafting wax, tree dressing, or electrical tape to seal out air. Allow the covering to wear away on its own. This surgery slows down the growth of the tree and makes the tree bear fruit at a younger age.

Pear Trees

Pear trees produce their fruit solely on spurs rather than branches. They grow slowly and need less pruning than fruit trees that bear fruit on limbs. According to *The History of Pear Trees* by Patrick Malcolm, it is believed that prehistoric man ate pears in Europe. Records also show that the pear tree made its way to

New England in 1629. Pear trees are medium sized, growing about 15 to 30 feet tall and 10 to 20 feet wide. Like apple trees, they need to cross-pollinate in order to produce fruit. People consider pear trees one of the easiest varieties of fruit trees to grow because they can grow well in a wide range of climates. A pear tree can start producing fruit within two to four years. Pear trees need full sun, especially morning sun, and they do well in well-drained, sandy soil.

If you are planting a young tree, start with a tree about 2 years old. You may need to stake it at first in order for it to withstand windy conditions. Prune the tree to have a central leader — you can switch to a modified central leader after a few years, if you prefer. You will want to thin out any excess branches to encourage your tree to grow in a spreading branch position. Also, pear trees tend to grow upright with several tops you need to cut off, except for the central leader. This will help to avoid the occurrence of narrow crotches that can break easily when loaded with fruit. In addition, remove any cross branches or those growing too close together or rubbing against each other. Do your pruning in late winter or early spring when the tree is still dormant and before new growth begins.

As your pear tree matures, you will find you will wind up pruning for fruit rather than branch positioning. You will want to do this because fruit seeds produce auxins that will affect subsequent growth. The larger the crop, the fewer the flower buds that will produce the next year's crop. By pruning off developing fruit, you even out fruit production from year to year. Otherwise, you will wind up with a large crop one year and a small crop the next.

Also, thin out any stems growing too densely, and pull off water sprouts immediately. If any limbs appear weak with spindly stems growing on the undersides, remove those limbs also to prevent the growth of poor-quality fruit. Also, remove dead branches that can leave your tree open to disease and insect infiltration.

Once your tree produces fruit, you must thin out the fruit so each pear is about 5 inches apart in order to stimulate and make room for the growth of younger spurs and new fruit. Otherwise, as your tree ages, you will wind up with too many spurs and less production of fruit. Also, if you pick off some of the fruit when the fruit is small and new, you will encourage your tree to produce larger fruit as a result. Remove crowded spurs, as well as older spurs.

One aspect that is nice about pear trees — in addition to being easier to grow — is they are less susceptible to the insects and diseases that often plague other fruit trees. At one time, pear trees were highly susceptible to fire blight, a destructible disease of apple and pear trees caused by a bacterium that turns the leaves black and kills the branches. But today, there are fire-blight-resistant varieties of pear trees, and arborists also have a better understanding of the disease. You should still stay on the lookout if you own a pear or apple tree. It makes the branches and leaves appear as if they have been held over a flame. You need to remove these branches immediately and then dispose of them at a safe distance in order to keep this disease from spreading. Also, make sure you sterilize your tools when you are done pruning in order to keep from spreading this disease to other parts of the tree and to other trees.

Plum Trees

Plum trees, which are native to the United States, Europe, Japan, and China, are considered small trees because they rarely exceed 20 feet tall. This makes them good for a small garden area or yard, especially since they are self-pollinating so you do not need to plant more than one. They do require regular pruning since their brittle wood, if left unattended, can weaken the tree. Plum  trees are known as stone fruit trees and grow best in Zones 5 to 7. They require a well-drained soil so use mulch when possible to help the soil retain its moisture.

There are several varieties of plums, which differ in size, flavor, and color, including reds, blues, purples, yellows, and greens. Plums can also range from bushes to trees. People prune plum trees to have an open center or modified central leader form. Once pruned to either form, plum trees require little pruning. Most plum trees produce fruit on spurs, although the Japanese plum tree grows on year-old stems as well. You want to prune so the plant receives light in the center, which is why the open center is often the popular form of choice — plum trees tend to have a scraggly way of growing.

Begin with a 1-year-old whip if you can, which ranges from 4 to 7 feet tall, particularly if you are growing a European or American plum variety. If you are planting a Japanese variety, then plant a 2-year-old, slightly branched tree. Cut the whips back to about a third, to a fat bud, and then cut off a third of the side branches.

When pruning a plum tree, always do it in June. Unlike most other trees pruned in late winter or early spring when the tree is dormant, plum trees are pruned in June because they grow strongly at that time. Plum trees are also susceptible to silver leaf disease in winter, which is a fungus that attacks its leaves.

In the second year after planting, trim the main stem back to about 18 inches, just above a bud. You should have three or four buds below this cut from the previous year. Pinch any side shoots to about six leaves to encourage fruit to grow the following year. When the central stem grows to about 8 feet high, prune it back to old wood above the highest limb.

In the third year, prune the leading shoots back to 12 inches from their main stems, and prune other shoots back to 6 inches from their main stems. By the fourth year and after, prune all leading shoots back by a third, and prune other shoots to 6 inches from their main stems. Cut off all diseased and dead wood, as well as branches that cross or rub against each other. You should leave the center open so it receives plenty of light and air.

Plums are also susceptible to a disease called black knot, where an abnormal, discolored growth forms along the branch twigs. You must remove these twigs immediately to stop the spread of the disease. Also, plum trees tend to have roots that grow close to the surface, which produces many suckers you will need to remove.

Like many fruit trees, plum trees can produce fruit erratically, producing a large crop one year and a small crop the next. To ensure a good crop every year, thin out the fruit when the tree has a large crop so the plums can grow without touching each other, about 5 inches apart. Unlike other fruit trees, you do not have to thin plum tree fruit unless you want a consistent yield each year. If you have a Japanese plum tree, the fruit will be larger and heavier so you may want to thin the fruit to 5 inches apart in order to prevent branches from breaking under the weight. If you want to keep your tree or bush small, you will need to do some heavy pruning, which the plum tree or bush can easily handle.

Nectarine Trees

The nectarine tree is a form of peach tree, but the fruit is smooth and firm, whereas the peach fruit is downy. Some call the nectarine a fuzzless peach. In fact, the nectarine

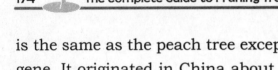

is the same as the peach tree except it is missing the fuzzy gene. It originated in China about 2,000 years ago, where it spread to ancient Persia (Iran), Greece, and Rome. The Spanish introduced it to the New World.

If you plan to grow a nectarine tree, keep in mind that it is a short-lived tree, averaging about a 12-year lifespan. Because it is related to the peach, your nectarine tree could possibly bear peaches and visa versa. The only way to guarantee it will bear nectarines is to grow a tree that has nectarine branches grafted on to a peach tree. Nectarines are self-pollinating so you only need one tree in your garden to reap fruit. As with peach trees, you must pick the fruit of a nectarine tree when ripe because they do not ripen well once harvested. Nectarine trees tend to grow quickly on their own, but pruning makes them grow even faster. The average height of a nectarine tree is 8 to 20 feet tall.

Nectarine trees need more pruning than other fruit trees because they produce fruit on year-old branches. Heavy pruning will encourage the growth of new wood, which in turn will yield more fruit so you must remove the previous year's growth. But, fruit will grow on the previous year's wood so leave enough to ensure a good crop. The best time to prune a nectarine tree is in late winter, when the tree is dormant and will not bleed. You can perform light-maintenance pruning to remove diseased or dead wood or manage growth in the summer.

When planting a nectarine tree, prune your whip so it will develop three to five lateral branches. If your tree's trunk is less than □ of an inch in diameter, cut your tree back to 18 to 24 inches above the ground. If it is larger, leave three to five well-placed lateral branches cut back 2 to 3 inches to stimulate growth, and remove any other remaining branches. Wait until the following winter when the tree is dormant to begin to shape your tree. Nectarine trees do best when they have an open center where air and light can get at the center of the tree and reach the lower branches. Once you have selected the branches you want to keep for your form, cut these branches back 2 to 3 feet from the trunk, and remove any other branches.

In your tree's second winter, you will want to encourage the development of secondary lateral branches. Pick two or three healthy branches growing outward from your primary limbs, and cut these back 2 to 3 feet, leaving small shoots and twigs along the branch. Remove any other secondary branches. Make sure when choosing your branches, you do not allow your nectarine tree to branch too close to the ground because this tree is prone to trunk borers.

In the following winter, you will work on creating your open center form. Since nectarines grow on the previous year's wood, remove excessive growth along the branches, but keep enough wood to produce the year's crop. A good rule of thumb is to prune 60 percent of your tree. This may seem excessive and your tree may look as if it has been scalped, but nectarines can handle hard pruning with ease because it results in a bumper harvest the next year. Also, remove growth at the top of the tree to prevent your tree from getting top heavy with fruit and to encourage your tree to grow taller.

Whenever you are pruning your nectarine tree, look carefully for fruit buds and be careful of cutting off any buds that will produce the following year's fruit. Prune the branches that are crossing or rubbing and dead or diseased. Also, look for any new growth that looks weak, and cut it off. On the remaining branches, try to stagger them. In other words, cut the limbs back to different lengths. For example, prune some branches back a quarter of the way, some a third of the way, and some half of the way. This encourages new fruitwood to form throughout the crown and not just at the tip of branches.

If space is limited, you can grow a dwarf nectarine tree, which grows 5 to 10 feet high. In addition, nectarines grow easily from pits if you want to start a plant from scratch. A good idea is to grow a nectarine from a fruit you have purchased from a local farmer's market. This way, you will know exactly what kind of nectarine tree you are growing, and you will ensure it is suitable for your particular climate and soil. If you choose to grow a nectarine from scratch, you will need to remove the seeds from the pit. Then, place the seeds in a plastic bag or sealed container, and put them in your refrigerator for four months to mimic the cold weather they need to germinate. About two months before the last spring frost, take your seeds out, and soak them overnight. Place them in a jar or pot, cover them with moist soil, and put them back in your fridge. Check every week for roots, and once the roots have sprouted, you can plant your seeds in the ground, provided that the frost period is over, or simply plant them in a pot until a whip grows tall enough to plant in the ground. Then, simply follow the pruning rules mentioned earlier in this chapter.

Citrus Trees

Citrus trees are bushy evergreen trees that need little pruning because they grow in the hottest parts of the United States and the world. Trees in northern climates need pruning to let in sunlight, but citrus trees get plenty of light year round. They are popular landscape choices if you live in California, Florida, and along the Gulf because they thrive in warm weather. You perform most of the pruning when a citrus tree is young and needs to be trained for a certain form. If you prune too much, it will take at least two years for your tree to bear fruit again. Also, pruned citrus bark is sensitive to the hot sun so you will need to cover it with white paint to prevent the bark from blistering. The best time to prune citrus trees is in spring because you have passed any chance of an occasional frost. If your tree is an older citrus and is not producing fruit, it can be reborn with extensive pruning. This means removing all wood thicker than 1 to 1 ½ inches in diameter, known as "skeletonizing" the tree.

Grapefruit trees

Grapefruit trees produce an abundance of fruit, which makes them a favorite because like all citrus, they are self-pollinating. Grapefruit trees are one of the newest additions to the citrus fruit family, which, according to  James MacFadyen in his 1837 book *Flora of Jamaica*, is actually a cross between the pummelo and the orange. Grapefruit nurseries did not take hold in the United States until the 1860s.

Grapefruit trees average a height of 15 to 20 feet and have well-rounded tops of spreading branches. The fruit's pulp can range in color from pale yellow or almost white to pink to deep red. It does best in Zones 9 to 11 with acidic limestone soil, which is why Florida is the largest producer of grapefruit in the United States.

Like most citrus trees, grapefruits need minimal pruning because the more leaves on the grapefruit tree, the more fruit it can produce. But, occasional pruning — about every two years — will help your tree produce the most fruit possible. If your tree is producing too much fruit at one time, then thin out the fruit while they are still small.

The best time to prune grapefruit trees is mid-spring to midsummer, from about late March to late July.

If you are planting a grapefruit tree, make sure you plant it in an area of your garden that receives a lot of sun and where the soil drains well. Grapefruit trees do best with open centers so gently remove any branches that do not fit this form. Other than that, a young grapefruit tree needs little pruning. You will need to protect it from possible frosts by draping a blanket or tarp over the young tree.

As your grapefruit tree matures, you will do most of the pruning to maintain its manicured look and to cut off dead or diseased wood. With grapefruit trees, you only need to cut off the dead part of the branch, not the entire branch.

Begin by examining your tree from all sides, and remove any shoots growing off the trunk. Since these shoots can be thorny, wear gloves to protect your hands. Also, remove any dead or insect-infested branches you see.

Next, remove any crisscrossed branches and branches growing too close together. Create an open center to let in air and light and to prevent the fungus that can plague grapefruit trees because of the moist climates they grow in. Also, prune thin branches growing from the sides and top of the tree to keep your plant looking neat and tidy. This will also keep its canopy to a minimum, which can prevent sunlight from reaching its core branches.

If you are removing large branches, make your first cut 15 inches out from the trunk of the tree. Begin the cut on the underside of the branch, sawing halfway through the branch. Then, make the top cut 18 inches out from the trunk, and saw at an angle until your cut meets the first cut on the underside. Your branch should fall off, leaving a nub. Remove this by cutting at an angle from the top of the nub to the trunk of the tree.

If you are trying to rejuvenate an old tree, cut back branches by a third. This will cause the grapefruit tree's root system to send energy into replacing the tree's canopy. It is not unusual for an old tree that is pruned to produce an abundance of fruit the following year.

Orange trees

Orange trees, with their white blossoms and bright-colored fruit, are one of the most attractive fruit trees for your garden. In addition, they have a wonderful smell. They grow on average about 20 feet tall with small, rounded heads. They need minimal care, like most citrus trees, but they do require full sun and well-drained soil. They grow best in Zones 9 to 11, and you need to cover them if you experience a cold snap.

You should not pick oranges until you are ready to eat them because they do not continue to ripen once picked and will spoil. The orange tree most likely originated in China, were brought to Europe, and then brought to

America. Many varieties of oranges exist, but the two main types include the navel and the Valencia. Navel oranges are best for eating, while Valencia oranges are used for juice. Tangerines are actually mandarin oranges, though not all mandarins are tangerines.

Orange trees are fairly easy to grow if you live in the right climate because they are self-forming and do not need pruning when young in order to shape them. You do need to remove water sprouts, as well as any branches less than 1 foot from the ground. In addition, remove any dead or diseased wood that will attract insect infestations.

You only need to prune orange trees, on average, every other year. The best time to prune is late January to late March. You want to do your pruning before the blossoms appear. As stated, you want to remove any suckers, low-reaching branches, and dead or diseased wood. You also want to cut off any branches that cross each other, grow too close together, or rub against each other. Also, remove any branches from the middle of the tree to create an open center. Like grapefruit, orange trees are prone to fungus so you want plenty of light and air to hit the center of the tree. Keep the wounds from any removed branches shaded from the sunlight in order to prevent sunburn. The best way to do this is to not remove any upper branches unless absolutely necessary.

Lemon trees

The lemon tree is one of the most popular types of citrus trees because of its color, taste, and smell. A lemon tree averages 10 to 20 feet in height and has sharp thorns on its branches. It is the most acidic of citrus fruit trees and can tolerate frost more than other citrus tree.

No evidence of the origin of the lemon tree exists, although people have linked its beginnings to northwestern India. The Spaniards brought it to the New World. Today, in the United States, lemons are mostly grown in Florida, Arizona, and California because these trees need a warm climate, in Zones 9 to 11, to survive.

Lemon trees can tolerate poor, sandy soil, but it requires well-drained soil and full sun. They enjoy a longer life than most citrus trees, averaging about 30 years. Lemon trees are considered low maintenance because they need very little pruning compared to other types of trees, although more pruning than most citrus trees. A lemon tree actually does better when left to shape itself. But like all trees, you must prune your lemon to remove dead or diseased wood and to encourage fruit production. Make sure to wear gloves because the branches have sharp thorns.

If you are planting a young, bare-rooted lemon tree, you will need to severely cut it back at planting time. Although a lemon tree does well when left to shape itself, you want to encourage it to grow with an open center. This guarantees adequate light and air in the center of the tree and prevents an environment where fungus can form. In the long run, it will also allow the tree's fruit to ripen better.

Although citrus trees are low maintenance and do not need pruning as often as other types of trees, lemon trees require more pruning than other citrus trees, about every two years. Lemon trees, unlike other citrus trees, grow in a long stem pattern that can easily break under the weight of their fruit. You will want to prune these back.

The best time to prune your lemon tree is at the end of winter or the beginning of spring. You want to do it before new buds form. First look for any dead branches — on the lemon tree, these will be dark brown or black. Only remove the part of the branch that has darkened, not the entire branch. Also remove branches from the center of the tree, since the open center form is best for lemon trees. Next, remove any branches crossing or rubbing against each other. Prune back the remaining branches about a third in height.

When pruning, keep in mind that lemons, as all citrus trees, flower and fruit on the current year's growth. If you feel your tree is bearing too much fruit, growing too closely together, and is straining its branches, thin them out when the fruit is still small. Do not forget to also remove any suckers and water sprouts draining energy from your lemon tree.

This person is pruning their lemon tree in March.

Lime trees

Lime trees are in the citrus family and are like lemons, only smaller, growing only 6 to 13 feet tall. Also, the size of the fruit is smaller, with lemons being around 4 to 5 inches in length and limes being about 3 inches long. Lime trees have a stronger scent than lemon trees and cannot handle the cold as easily as some lemon trees can, which is why lime trees are not native to the United States and instead originated in tropical climates.

Here, you can see the thorns on the branch of the lime tree.

Lime trees have thorny stems so wear gloves when pruning. You need to prune lime trees every two years, but they are quite resilient, being able to withstand too much pruning. If your tree is less than 4 feet tall, you can hold off on pruning. Once it is taller, the best time to prune is early spring and late summer, before the tree blooms or once the fruit is off the tree. As with other citrus plants, remove the suckers and water sprouts that can drain energy from the tree and zap fruit production. Next, remove any weak, damaged, or diseased branches and limbs that rub or cross each other. Also, try to create an open center, since this is the best form for any citrus tree because it allows air and sunlight to reach the center of the tree, increasing fruit production. If your lime tree's top canopy is top heavy, prune it back to create more balance.

When your tree starts bearing fruit, look for clusters when they are about the size of a grape. Remove all of the limes, except for one in each cluster. This will help your tree to produce fewer, larger limes that have better flavor.

Other Types of Fruit Trees

Many people feel intimidated by fruit trees and shrubs because they are afraid of pruning off the wrong branch, causing irreversible damage. Even if you did prune off a main branch, your tree or bush will probably grow a new one nearby in its place. Just take your time and study your plant, making sure to step back after each cut to view your specimen.

Often, fruit trees start out producing a large harvest when they are young because they have fewer branches so the fruit receives a lot of sunlight. But as the tree matures and grows more limbs, the crop can decrease in size and amount. Pruning fruit trees, therefore, helps to produce a larger yield. It also helps keep the amount of fruit produced consistent from year to year.

Berry-producing shrubs, on the other hand, need little pruning, except to remove dead or diseased branches and to shape your bush or keep it a certain size. Many berry-producing shrubs are unisexual so you will need to plant both males and females if you hope to harvest fruit.

Pawpaw trees

Pawpaw trees are small, tropical fruit trees native to the southern and mid-Atlantic United States that grow to about 15 feet tall. They do best when grown in full sun and have a pyramid shape with branches reaching down to the ground. Because the pawpaw tree is a compact tree in its size and root system, you can plant it near any structure without worry. Should you plant your tree in shade, it will grow

Pawpaw tree bloom

wider and will not have lower branches, but if newly planted, you should create some kind of partial shading for your pawpaw during the first two years. After that, your pawpaw will be ready to bear, and then it requires full sun if you want to reap a bounty of fruit.

You will need to plant two pawpaw trees, since they need cross-pollination in order to produce fruit, which look like short, fat bananas. What complicates this process is that pawpaw trees are not pollinated by bees because pawpaw trees have been around longer than bees. Instead, carrion flies and beetles pollinate them. While this is the natural way, if you really want to reap a bumper crop, you will have to pollinate by hand using an artist's paintbrush. You will have to collect the pollen from a different variety of pawpaw tree, and then brush the pollen on the flowers of the other tree before that tree shows any pollen. Pawpaw trees do well in acidic soil and will bear fruit when they are about 6 feet tall at about 5 to 6 years of age.

Pawpaw trees need little pruning beyond the training stage. But, it is important to remove any dead, damaged, or diseased branches on your pawpaw tree. If a branch is thick, place your saw where the branch meets the trunk. Make sure to cut at a 45-degree angle so water does not pool in the cut and cause disease or attract insects. If you are simply removing old growth in order to stimulate fruit production, only prune off the old wood on the branch, and leave any new buds and growth. Other than that, the only pruning you may want to do is on the top canopy in order to keep the fruit within reach. If you choose to prune the top, do it in midsummer. Pawpaw trees are also prone to suckers at the roots that grow some distance from the actual trunk. You will want to remove these immediately because the suckers will grow into a thicket. Your pawpaw tree will produce fruit in clusters on stems that grew during the previous season. Prune when your tree is dormant in order to stimulate growth.

Persimmon trees

Persimmon trees are deciduous fruit trees native to the United States. Their barks resemble an alligator hide, and their fruit resemble under-ripe tomatoes or small,  golden plums, which were favorites among Native Americans. The persimmon tree grows an average height of 30 to 70 feet and 25 feet wide with drooping branches and bears fruit for up to 50 years or more. It does best when grown in Zones 5 to 9, although some varieties can grow in Zone 4. It grows well in climates that have moderate winters and mild summers. The fruit is also a favorite among wild birds and animals so make sure to pick the crop once it starts to ripen, and put the fruit in a window to finish ripening. Unripened persimmon fruit can be toxic to some animals.

If you are growing a persimmon tree, plant it when the tree is still a sapling. But, you will need to plant several if you wish to reap fruit because it is difficult to determine a persimmon tree's sex, and 90 percent of persimmons are female. Your trees will need plenty of sunlight and soil rich in nutrients. Make sure to water it well for the first few years. Persimmon trees are not prone to disease or insect infestation.

Fruit tree enthusiasts love persimmon trees for more than their tasty fruit. A persimmon tree needs minimal maintenance, with pruning once a year suggested in its early years in order to shape your tree. An open center or modified central leader form is best so air and light can reach the fruit hidden in the drooping branches. In addition, during the first year, only prune crossed or damaged branches. During the second year, cut your tree back so it is only 2 to 3 feet tall and forms a vase-like shape.

Do not let your persimmon tree bear fruit until it is at least 4 years old. If it bears fruit too soon, it will weaken the tree, and it will not bear fruit again for many years. During the first few years, pinch off all fruit in the summer. Once your tree bears fruit, do your pruning in late winter or early spring in order to stimulate the buds. Only prune in summer if you are trying to control your tree's growth. Look for any damaged branches — high winds can damage brittle persimmon branches. Also, cut off any branches that cross or rub and any diseased or dead. You will also need to prune to expose any branches that bear fruit but are shaded from the sun. Prune back problem branches to the third bud inside the tree. Trim back the remaining branches a third to the bud that faces the direction you want your limb to grow. Prune so there is about 1 foot between branches to increase sunlight. Remove any stubs to prevent new growth on them. Do not forget to remove suckers and water sprouts all year as they appear.

Fig trees

Fig plants are ancient plants great for the garden because you can grow them as either a bush or a tree. The average height of a fig tree ranges between 25 to 40 feet. If your garden space is limited, you can still enjoy this fruit tree by pruning it into a small shrub or even keeping it in a pot, since fig tree roots do not mind confined spaces and will still produce a large crop of fruit. Also, if you

have cold winters, a severe winter can kill a single trunk so a bush or potted fig is preferred in this type of climate.

If you grow your fig as a tree, train it to have an open center. If you live where the sun is intense, train it to have a modified central leader form so the branches can prevent sunburn. A fig plant bears fruit on both the previous year's wood and on the current year's growth. Some varieties of fig trees need pollination from a certain type of wasp, while others do not require pollination to bear fruit.

The best time to prune a fig tree is in late fall or on frost-free days in winter when fig trees are dormant because fig trees tend to bleed. If you are planting a young fig, prune it back by half to allow the plant to focus its energy on developing its roots and to grow side branches that make it fuller.

In the following winter after planting, prune your tree for fruiting wood. Choose four to six branches, and remove the rest. This is also a good time to remove any dead or diseased branches and any suckers growing from the root base. Next, trim off any secondary branches growing off your main branches at less than a 45-degree angle. Finally, cut back the main branches by a third to a fourth. This will allow your tree to direct its energy toward producing fruit in the next year.

For mature fig plants, prune back branches about 1 foot each year to stimulate new growth and to prevent crowding of branches. Also, thin out the crown, but try not to make too many head cuts. If you want your fig tree or shrub to produce a large crop, in the summer, pinch off the tip after 1 foot of growth from the previous season. In addition, prune the roots because this will also promote fruiting.

Blueberry bushes

The blueberry is a flowering plant mainly native to North America, South America, Europe, and Asia. It can vary in size from 3 to 160 inches in height, and it can take years to come into full-fruit production. The smaller plants are wild and are known as lowbush blueberries, whereas those  grown commercially or in gardens are known as highbush blueberries. Some varieties are evergreens, while others are deciduous. The fruit is a small berry, and the blueberry bush bears fruit from May to August, depending on the climate and altitude where it grows.

Most fruiting shrubs do not need extensive pruning, and the blueberry bush is no different, although it does need pruning annually to shape it and to remove dead or damaged branches. Blueberry bushes, in fact, are fairly simple to grow and maintain. Pruning helps to stimulate the plant's fruit production and ensures an annual crop. Blueberry bushes grow from new stems that sprout from the crown of the shrub each year. Its branches do not live long, but with annual pruning, you can ensure that your blueberry bush does.

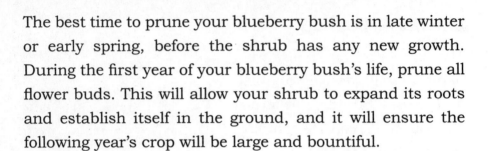

The best time to prune your blueberry bush is in late winter or early spring, before the shrub has any new growth. During the first year of your blueberry bush's life, prune all flower buds. This will allow your shrub to expand its roots and establish itself in the ground, and it will ensure the following year's crop will be large and bountiful.

Blueberry bushes bear fruit in late summer or fall so in winter or late spring, prune back branches so air and light can reach the center of the plant. But do not prune too much or cut back more than one-third of the previous season's growth. Also, remove any dead, diseased, broken, or weak limbs, as well as any lower branches close to the ground. The idea is to allow as much sunlight as possible to reach the fruit throughout the shrub.

If your bush is more than 4 years old and dense, you will need to thin it out so enough air and light can reach the fruit buried in the bush and to get rid of sterile branches more than 4 years old that no longer bear fruit. Also, trim the branches back to the height you want your shrub. Get rid of any excessively long stems or those that have more than five buds in order to prevent the branches from weakening because of an overload of blueberries. But be careful — do not prune off more than half of the latest growth, and always cut just above an outside bud or branch. Also, only remove the weakest branches, and leave the strongest ones. The amount of pruning you need to do on your blueberry bush will vary from year to year, depending on the amount of growth, fruit production, and which — if any — branches are weak, dead, or diseased. Do not forget to always remove any suckers growing near the base of the bush.

If you have an older and neglected blueberry bush, you can renovate the plant. Simply cut the whole shrub down to the ground during its dormant season. This will cause your bush to put out new sprouts so you will need to thin these out. This drastic measure will cause your shrub to stop producing fruit for at least a year, but the tradeoff is that you will have a viable blueberry shrub once again.

Apricot trees

Apricot trees originated in China and then spread to Asia. The Romans are thought to have brought them to Europe, where they were then brought to North America. In the United States,  apricot trees grow best on the Pacific coast, but certain varieties do well in the southern Midwest and in the East. They are easy to grow and do not take up a lot of space, since they only reach heights of 12 to 18 feet and widths of 6 to 10 feet. They are also self-pollinating so you only need one tree to reap its tasty fruit. They are sensitive to heat so they do best in partial shade and well-drained soil.

Apricot trees are susceptible to disease so prune them prior to new growth in the early spring. They also bear fruit earlier than most fruit trees, in early summer on wood that is 1 to 3 years old so you will need to prune enough to stimulate new growth each year. This does not mean you have to prune drastically; light tip pruning should do the trick. Also, cut away old, diseased, or damaged wood. In most cases, fruit thinning is not necessary, but if you do prune your tree severely, your tree will bear less fruit that is larger in size. Keep the spacing between fruit about 2 inches apart.

If you are training a young tree, the best forms are an open center or modified central leader so plenty of light and air reaches all of its branches. Cut your new tree to about 24 to 36 inches tall. If you are pruning for the open center form, remove any central branches, and keep four or five equal branches set wide apart. If you are creating a modified central leader, locate the leader twig. If your tree has two leaders, remove the less dominant one about a ¼ inch from where it joins the other leader. Next, prune off any branches that have a narrow crotch of less than 45 degrees from the main trunk. Then, pick four or five branches you want as the main branches or "ribs" of your tree. Severely cut these back to a ¼ inch above one live but dormant bud. Your tree will look sparse. Do not prune any other branches during the first year.

During the second year, repeat the same pruning as the first; that is, prune off any new twigs and water sprouts, particularly those growing in the center of the tree because you want to have an open center or modified central leader. Also, prune any branches growing downward and any limbs that rub or cross each other. Prune any side branches longer than 30 inches back by 10 inches. Make these cuts a ¼ inch above a lower dormant bud. Also, remove any suckers growing at the base of the trunk.

Once your tree matures, after the second year, continue to prune any dead, damaged, or diseased branches. Also, prune any water sprouts and branches growing downward. You want your apricot tree to grow outward and upward. Lightly tip prune your tree every third year. If the bud clusters on a branch die, cut the branch back by 6 to 12 inches to stimulate new growth. Do this every third year.

Most importantly, try not to overly prune your apricot, since apricot trees are susceptible to a number of diseases, and pruning more than every three years opens your tree up to disease. When you do prune, remove 20 percent of the previous years' growth.

Cherry trees

Cherry trees are not the easiest trees to grow in your garden because they are fussy and sensitive to climate change. A cherry tree is a deciduous tree that does not do well in long periods of hot weather, and

they must have a cold winter to bear fruit. Another pro — or con, depending on how you look at it — is that cherry trees attract birds. This means you can enjoy a wide variety of wild birds that will flock to your tree, but the birds may eat up your crop. You can cover your tree with a net to keep out the birds.

Cherry trees grow on average about 6 to 35 feet tall and 8 to 40 feet wide, depending on the variety you grow. Cherry trees are related to plum trees, but the fruit is smaller. They originated in China, but now, North Africa, most of Asia, and Europe, as well as North America, have them. Most varieties do best in Zones 4 through 8 and live an average of 20 years.

Your cherry tree must have well-drained soil because it will not do well if its roots are constantly wet. Your tree will also need full sun. Wild cherries, which taste sour, can self-pollinate, but sweet cherries need another tree in order to bear fruit. Plant your trees 18 feet apart. If your tree is young, it will take two years for it to bear fruit, and you will need to prune carefully in order not to remove the spurs that produce the fruit. Cherry trees do best with a central leader or a modified central leader because they do not do well with the extensive pruning involved in creating an open center form. A central leader is really the best choice because it makes for a stronger tree, but with a cherry tree, you sometimes have to switch to a modified leader as it ages simply because of the cherry tree's natural growth pattern. In addition, cherry trees tend to grow into a bushy form even with the best of pruning intentions so you will need to train your tree early, or it will grow too wide, and its branches will grow too close to the ground.

Begin to train your tree a year after planting. Choose your main branches, and thin out all the others. Choose your main branches carefully, and do not choose branches growing directly opposite each other because the fruit can be heavy, and the weight can split the trunk.

Your tree will bear fruit on 2- to 10-year-old spurs so once it begins to bear fruit, thin out old spurs from time to time. You can easily identify the old spurs because of their aging appearance. Also, prune off any dead or diseased branches, as well as limbs damaged by weather. This will direct the tree's energy into the healthy branches and into producing fruit. Remove any suckers at the base of the tree, as well as any water sprouts growing from the trunk or branches. When removing branches, cut them at an angle about an $\frac{1}{8}$ inch above a bud.

You must prune a cherry tree once every year, or it will die of starvation because it cannot handle the unfettered growth. You must prune your tree carefully because unlike some trees, a cherry tree is sensitive to drastic pruning. The best time to prune is in summer, after you have picked your fruit because in winter, when most deciduous trees are pruned, cherry trees can contract silver leaf. Always prune to an outward-facing bud so any new growth will not crowd the center of the tree.

If you are trying to restore an older or neglected cherry tree, do your pruning gradually. Begin by cutting back the leader, and then cut the upper branches about 2 feet shorter than the leader. In the spring, choose which branches you want to remain, and thin out the others. Leave any healthy lower limbs, but prune branches too low to the ground. The next year, thin out any new growth at the top of the tree so the lower limbs and fruit can receive adequate light.

The Fruit Tree Espalier

Fruit trees do well when pruned to an espalier form, an artistic form of pruning that creates a two-dimensional plant sometimes used when spacing is minimal. An **espalier** is a tree or shrub grown flat against a wall, fence, building, or trellis. According to *The Pruning Book* by Lee Reich, espalier plants originated in Europe in the 16th century as a way to train fruit trees to grow on walls in order to take advantage of the land along the walls and the extra warmth generating from them.

If this is a form you would like to use for your fruit tree, make sure you choose a spot that does not receive direct sunlight all day because walls reflect heat, which can cause your fruit tree's leaves and fruit to suffer in warm weather. If possible, also choose a white wall because white absorbs little heat, whereas a dark wall will attract it. If you live in cool weather, choose a spot that receives a lot of sunlight and has a dark wall as the backdrop. Also, make sure you plant your tree 6 to 10 inches away from the wall or fence so it receives proper air circulation.

The espalier form is often chosen when a fruit tree may struggle if grown in the open where, for reasons such as spacing or lack of sunlight or too much sunlight, it may make it difficult or impossible for the tree to bear fruit. Fruit trees as espaliers can be both productive and attractive. If your espalier fruit tree is sheltered, its fruit will ripen earlier than fruit trees grown out in the open. Another benefit of the espalier fruit tree is that every stem produces fruit that, thanks to the amount of sunlight and air, is larger, tastier, and attractive.

Espaliers are not really as complicated as they may look. For one thing, their size is contained so you do not even need to drag out the ladder. Also, even though they require constant pruning, the cuts are small. When creating an espalier, keep in mind that your tree will have one or more main stems that are leaders, which will grow out of the trunk. It also has permanent stems, also known as arms or ribs, some of which grow out of the leader or leaders and some that do not. These arms are usually horizontal. If your espalier has ribs, these grow in a herringbone pattern off the leaders when you have a fan-shaped espalier. The goal of growing an espalier is to minimize the branch growth and maximize the fruit growth.

Different forms of espalier patterns exist, all of which can add an artistic flair to your garden. In fact, you can create your own pattern. Typical forms include the U-palmette, candelabra, horizontal palmette, double-U palmette, oblique palmette, wide U with horizontal palmettes, and fan. With an espalier, you want to develop stems having perfect symmetry with buds along the entire length. You will sometimes need to prune a whole branch, and sometimes you will only need to cut off a few inches of a branch or remove just the tip.

The fruit trees that make the best espalier include ones that bear fruit on spurs, such as apple cherry, nectarine, pear, fig, and plum trees. This is because in order to create an espalier, you have to remove many of the step tips and lateral branches, which are areas where many fruit trees that do not have spurs flower and fruit. Trees that bear fruit on spurs grow their spurs along the branches, which espalier training does not cut.

To begin training your espalier, plant your young fruit tree against your wall or fence, stake it, and then wait until the roots have established. You can also use a trellis instead of a stake and wire your trunk to the trellis instead of a stake. Once your roots are established, decide how wide you want your espalier, and insert posts on either end. Then, string galvanized wire between the two posts, crossing the original stake a few inches above the buds of the shoots growing from the sides of your tree.

Next, choose three of your tree's best shoots, and prune off the other shoots. Tie two of the horizontal shoots to the wire, and tie the vertical shoot or leader to the stake. You may want to use string instead of wire to attach your branches to the main wire because wire may cut into the bark. When the vertical shoot grows to your desired height, string a second wire to the two end posts. Now, you will need to select the three or four best top shoots, and tie them horizontally to the wire, just as you did with the first wire. Continue this process for a third wire — or fourth, depending on the height you have picked — to train new shoots, while pruning off any shoots not needed.

After a few years pass, the central trunk will be large and strong enough to support itself, and its support stake can then be removed. Continue pruning and training as needed each season. Prune the fruiting spurs when the tree is dormant in winter or early spring. Make sure your fruit is spaced well, and cut off any old spurs. If any shoots you have pruned the previous late summer or fall have grown again, prune those back. This is also a good time to cut back your horizontal branches.

It will take about three to four years for your espalier tree to mature. Branches not part of your espalier form will continuously need pruning off, but do this in the spring. Also, shape your espalier every month by removing branches and twigs not growing in the correct places. Espaliers take work, but the reward will be that you will reap larger and sweeter fruit thanks to added exposure to sunlight that your fruit will receive, and you will also garner an interesting focal point in your garden.

CASE STUDY: ADVICE FROM A PROFESSIONAL FRUIT TREE GROWER

LeeAnn Barton is a sales representative for Dave Wilson Nursery's New Mexico, Oklahoma, Texas, and East Point territories. She also teaches Dave Wilson Nursery's "Backyard Orchard Culture Techniques" to commercial and home gardening clientele.

Arborist techniques, as well as those taught on the college level, are not necessarily the best techniques for the backyard fruit grower. So, what we teach is what we at Dave Wilson Nursery call the "backyard orchard pruning techniques." It is a system that goes against what many teach about pruning, but we do it because home gardens are not orchards. The purpose of including fruit trees in the home garden is to grow fruit without hassle. Controlling a tree's size with summer pruning alleviates many problems. Standard orchard pruning techniques were developed for commercial orchards. When everyone lived in a farm-based society, pruning was delayed because people were too busy with harvest, preservation, and preparing for winter to prune. Even with an understanding of how thinning and pruning increased fruit production, other chores took priority on a homestead.

I tell people to find what works for them. A home gardener needs to ask what he or she wants — possibly a large tree, one to hang a swing from or sit under. Backyard orchard culture techniques bring the size of an average fruit tree down to a size where you can do all your pruning with just a set of loppers and hand shears, and you never need a ladder. This appeals to home gardeners.

These techniques are also geared to prevent injuries — both to the tree and to the gardener. One of the main ways people will injure a tree is they will cut close to the trunk or flush with the trunk, but you should never cut into the bud collar. Another tree injury I have seen has to do with the usually recommended open center method for most fruit trees. People are taught to prune to the outside bud to get the next branch to go in an outward fashion, but what I have seen is that the person will take that to the extreme and prune to a bud almost horizontal to the ground so as the tree grows and the branch matures, all the fruit and weight will cause the branch to break at the trunk union.

A much better approach is to prune branches to create a 45-degree angle between the trunk and scaffold branch. That way, the trunk supports the weight of the fruit and secondary branching. You still get an open center, but the trunk bears the weight of the fruit instead of the branch. You make your first scaffold branches grow at a 45-degree angle and gently grow to an outward spread instead.

As far as injuries to people, here is a good example: I bought a house that had an old apple tree probably 30 feet tall, and even on an 8-foot ladder with an extended pole saw, I could still not reach far enough. It was very frustrating that I could not bring the canopy down to a workable height and had to have an arborist come to handle it. But, I have pruned a lot from the ground, and when you work all day with a pole saw and your neck is leaning back and you are pulling with your arm, it is painful in the shoulders and the arm muscles, plus your neck, and of course, the unpleasantness of twigs and leaves falling in your face because I find it difficult to wear a full face shield.

Ladder injuries are another reason why I discourage letting a fruit tree's height get out of control, especially as you get older. We believe that not only do you not have to use a ladder, but also it is so much easier to detect disease if your tree is kept small. You can see what is going on before you just start spraying. Plus, if you are spraying, you have mist falling down on you. In orchards where the trees are large, they have a tanker truck to spray but that is not feasible for the home gardener. So, we advise keeping fruit trees small for the home garden.

Chapter 10:

Pruning Nut Trees

One of the nice things about nut trees is they grow easily from seed. If you plant a seed or buy a seedling from a nursery, expect to wait six to 12 years for it to bear fruit. Grafted nut trees take less time, and the nuts tend to be larger and easier to crack. In addition, grafted seedlings will bear nuts earlier than non-grafted ones and will produce a heavier crop than trees grown from seeds.

If you plant a seedling lightly branched, prune all the branches back to the first bud from the end, and cut the top back to the second bud from the top of the tree. You can also cut the branches back to the main stem and leave the top of the tree intact. If your whip has no branches, remove a third of the total length of the tree to just above a bud.

When nut trees grow wildly in the forest, they tend to lose their lower branches as the tree grows toward the sun. If your whip is a large, growing nut tree, you will want to train it to grow with a central leader. Prune all branches that will weaken your tree, such as long, heavy, horizontal branches that will put a strain on your young tree and eventually split off. Also, remove any branches rubbing other limbs or forming crotches less than 45-degree angles.

When your nut tree matures, continue to remove dead, diseased, or damaged branches, as well as limbs with heavy nut loads on weak crotches.

Pecan Trees

Pecan trees are native to the southern and southwestern parts of the United States. They are deciduous trees related to the hickory and can grow 66 to 130 feet tall. If you plant a pecan, make sure you have the room for it because their trunks can grow to 6 feet in diameter, and while each tree can grow both male and female flowers, they need another variety to pollinate. They can also live up to 300 years.

You should train young pecan trees to grow with a central leader and should prune them when the tree is dormant, in late winter, and past its fruiting time, which is October. You can grow them with a modified central leader, but a central leader is preferred because it makes for a stronger tree to hold the heavy nuts. If your tree has more than one leader, choose one, and remove the other. Upon planting your pecan tree, cut back the leader to half the size of the tree, usually about 36 to 42 inches tall.

Wait until the tree's first dormant period in late winter, and tip prune the leader. Next, decide which branches will be the main ones, tip prune those, and remove the others.

Choose carefully, since pecan trees have longevity and your choices will be apparent over decades. It is best to keep those branches that form wide angles with the central leader. In the first few years, tip prune the leader and side branches to shape your tree. You should also remove a few of its bottom branches each year so that over time your tree will eventually have a 6- to 8-foot, branch-free lower trunk. It should take about four to five years to completely shape your pecan tree. Other than occasionally removing dead, diseased, or damaged branches, as well as branches rubbing together or growing crooked — which you can remove any time of the year — your pecan tree will need little pruning during its lifetime.

Walnut Trees

The walnut tree originated in Persia (now Iran), where it made its way to England and then to the colonies. Walnut trees produce both male and female flowers and do best in a continuously warm climate. The male flowers grow off year-old wood, while the females form on new wood. They are drought resistant and are low-maintenance, since a mature walnut only requires occasional pruning.

When planting a young walnut tree, plant it 30 to 40 feet from other trees because walnut trees can grow to 60 feet tall and can live up to 300 years. You will want to plant your tree in spring, after the last frost. Choose a site that receives full sun and has well-drained soil. You can train walnut trees with an open center, central leader, or modified central leader form, but they will grow stronger and larger when formed with a central leader or modified central leader because the terminal bud is easily damaged by weather when the tree is young, which can result in an overgrowth of sprouts that can eventually turn your walnut tree into a bush. You will need to pinch and snip these sprouts continuously in your tree's early years to keep it with one main trunk. Also, upon first planting, cut your leader stem back about a third. Choose the tree's strongest branches as the scaffold branches, and remove the rest.

During the first few years, prune the scaffolding branches back by removing the tips, and prune off branches crossing or rubbing against each other, as well as any damaged branches. You will also need to remove suckers that are prone to grow at the root base. You also might want to stake your young tree, since nurseries sell most walnut trees grafted, making the young wood brittle and breakable at the graft.

In most trees, you would want to prune branches that have crotches at less than a 45-degree angle. But with walnut trees, there is less of a risk of crotched branches weakening the tree's health because this tree is made of hardy wood.

In fact, many people grow walnut trees for their wood rather than for their nuts. As your tree grows, you will want to remove any branches growing downward or any limbs that droop and, therefore, might break off because of a heavy load of nuts. Since walnut trees are great shade trees, prune lower branches so you have a space you can walk on underneath the tree about 6 to 8 feet.

Your walnut tree can start producing nuts when it is 6 years old, but it is not considered mature until 10 years old. Once your tree matures and starts producing nuts, prune it in early fall after you pick the nuts. Do not prune in spring because walnut trees tend to bleed badly then. You will need to prune your mature walnut tree annually to stimulate growth and to prevent the interior of the crown from becoming shaded, restricting nut production. Remove dead, diseased, or damaged branches or limbs crossing or rubbing against each other. You will also want to remove lower branches over time during the fall so you eventually have 9 feet of branchless trunk that will enable you to reap the full benefits of this shade tree.

Chestnut Trees

Chestnut trees are deciduous hardwood trees that can reach 100 to 130 feet high and up to 10 feet in diameter. The northeastern

part of the United States once contained bountiful American chestnut trees, but they were almost entirely wiped out in the early 1900s because of a chestnut blight, which is a fungal disease brought into the country on Asian chestnut tree imports. Today's variety is crossbred with imported chestnut trees to make them blight resistant, although there is a movement to restore the American chestnut tree across the United States. Chestnut trees bear three nuts in each green burr in late summer and early fall.

Chestnut trees can grow in Zones 4 through 8, but they do best in areas with hot summers. They grow rapidly and make great shade trees, but do not plant your tree near a patio of heavy foot traffic because they produce a large crop of nuts that fall to the ground. You also need to make sure you have plenty of space because chestnut trees are cross-pollinators so you will need to plant more than one tree in order to produce nuts. You need to plant your trees at least 35 feet apart. You also need to plant your tree in fast-draining clay soil.

Your chestnut tree will need a strong central leader with an equal number of branches on each side so train your young tree with a single trunk. Remove any lower branches below 5 feet on the trunk, as well as any suckers growing straight up or down. Lower branches and suckers will zap the tree of the energy it needs to grow tall and straight.

The nice part about a chestnut tree is that as it matures, it should only need minimal pruning. Prune only in the fall, and do not prune from April to July, when the tree will bleed heavily. Do not prune the top more than a third to a fourth back in any one year, or you could stunt or kill your tree, and do not prune any branches growing directly off the trunk, unless diseased or dead.

Chestnut trees bear flowers and nuts on new shoots in the second to tenth year. Encourage nut production by removing branches that cross or rub against each other, as well as any diseased or dead wood. Since the wood is brittle, it is also important to prune back long branches in order to prevent breakage that can open the tree to disease or insect infestation. Use a net to catch the nuts, since chestnut tree nuts are not picked; rather, the tree drops them to the ground. As your chestnut tree ages, you will discover it produces more nuts with every passing year.

Hazelnut Trees

Hazelnut trees, also known as filberts, are found all over North America, especially in Oregon and Washington, although Turkey is the world's largest producer. You can grow them as either trees or shrubs, although they are usually grown more as bushes rather than trees. If you grow your plant as a tree, the best form to train it in is with an open center. It adds a tasty addition to your garden, especially if space is limited, because hazelnut trees stay small at around 12 feet tall and 5 to 10 feet wide. In addition, you will need to plant more than one tree because hazelnuts need cross-pollination to bear nuts. If you have a grafted tree, you will need to stay on top of the suckers that will grow around the root base.

Hazelnut trees and bushes produce nuts in the fourth year. Mature hazelnut trees need little pruning, but it is important to prune in late fall, winter, or early spring when it is dormant. Prune back about a third of the branches, enough to stimulate the new growth needed for the following year's crop and also to keep your tree in shape. Remove old or dead branches, as well as those that cross or rub against each other or those damaged during the winter. You also might want to thin the top of the tree so the crop receives adequate air and light.

If your hazelnut is a bush, prune it to only five or six main stems. This will keep your shrub from getting too wide or turning into a thicket. In the 12th year, cut your bush to the ground in spring. You will not get any nuts that year, but your bush will come back healthier and hardier.

Let the nuts from your tree or bush fall to the ground rather than trying to pick them. Use a net to catch them because your tree or bush will produce a bounty of nuts.

Chapter 11

Pruning Hedges

The idea of a planting shrubs or trees to create a hedge or hedgerow goes back several thousand years to Roman times. They were popular in England when the government issued the Enclosure Acts, which allowed citizens to enclose their land with permission from the government. In 1836 and 1845, the government passed the General Enclosure Acts, which allowed citizens to enclose their land without government approval. People created hedges using thorny bushes and trees gathered from the English countryside. They carefully crafted these hedges by tying and twisting the limbs together so they formed an impenetrable barrier. Because the hedges were used in the countryside and space was not as big of an issue as it currently is, they were not always sheared back to a neat form. In the formal gardens of England under the reign of Queen Elizabeth I, **knot gardens** — made of a variety of tightly sheared shrubs — became popular. They are called knot gardens because when viewed from above, such as out of a castle

This English knot garden requires a significant amount of upkeep and labor.

window, the lines of tightly sheared shrubs seem to weave around each other, creating the appearance of a Celtic knot. Over time, as their designs became more elaborate, these famous knot gardens became difficult to maintain and required a staff of gardeners who did nothing all day but trim the hedges with manual shears. The size of plants used for knot gardens was much smaller than plants used in hedgerows because they had a purely ornamental purpose. Some of the European knot gardens, such as those found in France and England, are still around today, and their fantastic designs are still meticulously maintained.

If you would like to try your hand at making your own knot garden, be prepared to spend considerable time in keeping it neat and tidy. Knot gardens require daily clipping and trimming so you should only consider this undertaking if you have the time to devote to it. First, draw out a design on graph paper centering on a focal point in the garden, such as an interesting specimen plant, statue, or fountain. Choose plants that complement — they should be the same size at maturity and have similar leaf texture. These can include evergreen shrubs or hollies, for example. Shrubs that grow large, such as privet or boxwood, need more maintenance than low-growing bushes or herbs do, such as lavender or germander, which need pruning only two or three times a year. Keep in mind that some bushes die back in the winter and may leave your garden looking bare. Planting blooming plants with similar bloom times and colors will give the knot garden a sense of order. A row of shrubs having the same color blooms can have a dramatic impact. For example, use two or three different varieties of the same shrub that produce different color blooms, and plant one color per line. This creates the appearance of lines of color weaving under and over each other. Take your time laying out the garden to get the design just right, and use mulch or fine gravel to fill in the empty areas between lines in the design. Start small because you can always add on to your knot garden as the years pass. Do not limit yourself to permanent bushes or shrubs in your knot garden. You can lay out the planting beds in the desired pattern and fill them with your favorite vegetable plants.

In the United States, inexpensive fencing, drier climate, and the rapid advancement of settlers throughout the west prevented the idea of growing a hedge to hold livestock or to make a long-lasting knot garden to take hold. Nowadays, hedges are used exclusively in residential and commercial landscaping. The modern hedge is a mix of old hedgerows and the formal knot gardens. They designate a barrier, create a formal appearance, function as a backdrop for other plants, hide unsightly objects, create privacy, make a shelter for wildlife, create a windbreak, and occasionally create art. Of course, one hedge can serve all of these purposes at the same time. When creating a windbreak, which is a row of hedges or trees used to lessen or create a barrier to wind, remember that each foot of hedge height equals 10 feet of wind protection; an 8-foot hedge creates 80 feet of wind protection.

Large shears can be used to trim a hedge.

To shear a hedge or prune it into a nice neat shape, you have to keep an even line across the top going the entire time, and the bottom must be wider than the top so sunlight can reach the bottom branches of the hedge. If the top of the hedge is the same width or wider than the bottom, the bottom portion will eventually lose its leaves and become a collection of woody branches. Once you have woody branches at the bottom of the hedge, it is difficult to get them to green up again. The best way to ensure you continue to cut on the same level the entire time you prune a hedge is to set up posts on each end of the hedgerow, and tie a string between the posts. You can use a string level you hang on the string so you know when you are holding the string steady to get a perfect shear. String levels are really inexpensive, and you can pick one up at the same hardware or department store where you buy the string. After you cut across the top of the hedge, you can probably correctly estimate how to cut the sides and ends, as long as you keep in mind that the bottom must be wider than the top by just a few inches. The amount will differ depending on the height of the hedge after you make the top cut.

You should shear all hedges when they begin to look ragged. If you wait too long, you will expose woody stems when you shear it back, and you will create gaps along the hedgerow. You cannot maintain a formal hedge too much. The more you shear it and keep it in shape, the better it will look because the plant's energy and auxin levels can remain within the shrub and do not get wasted on growth you will cut away. In areas with heavy snowfall, shear the bushes into a rounded shape so heavy snow cannot accumulate and break branches, causing wounds that can damage or destroy the shrub. For a single specimen, shear in whatever way you desire, but once again, be sure you make the bottom slightly wider than the top.

The only exception to frequent shearing of a formal hedge is if the hedge consists of blooming plants. In that case, shear the hedge immediately after each bloom period. Shearing a blooming hedge freshens up the hedge, increases the level of green growth, and prevents the plants from using their energy to create seeds.

A well-kept hedge is an attractive way to add privacy to your property.

Hedgelaying

Hedgelaying, also called hedge pleaching, is an old method of managing hedges that creates an impenetrable wildlife or livestock barrier. Hedgelaying began in Roman times, but it became more popular during Saxon times of England as a way to keep livestock in and predators out. Pleaching hedges still serves those purposes, but it also provides a safe haven for wildlife. In fact, hedgelaying has experienced a surge in popularity in some areas because of its conservation benefits. *To learn about pleaching trees, see Chapter 7.*

It requires some thought and practice, but the idea behind hedgelaying is simple. You should cut large branches of robust, large shrubs at least 8 feet tall halfway through and lay them over each other all going in the same direction. Then, set upright posts along the sides of the laid branches. Tie the laid branches to the posts and to each other so they remain in place. This creates a tight fence animals cannot penetrate. Because the shrub branches are not completely cut through, not all branches die, and new growth sprouts along the branches that you then trim at the desired height after two years. As these branches become older and thicker, you can cut them halfway through and lay them the same way as the previous branches.

If you are preparing a hedge for hedgelaying, prune the side branches only for a few years prior to laying the hedge. This makes the hedgerow look like a long wall of green until it is successfully laid. You should practice hedgelaying in a rural setting because it can result in large sections of dead shrubs if not done correctly, which can appear unsightly if you have neighbors living nearby. But, it is an interesting and ancient way of managing hedges that is becoming lost in modern times because of its work-intensive requirements. A laid hedge is not only useful and beautiful, but it is also a valuable shelter for wildlife. A good hedgelayer is considered an artist in some parts of the world.

Popular Evergreen Bushes for Hedges

Some of the more popular evergreen bushes to use as hedges are:

- Boxwood (*Buxus* spp.).
- Privet (*Ligustrum* spp.).
- Holly (*Ilex* spp.).
- Canadian hemlock (*Tsuga Canadensis*).
- American arborvitae (*Thuja occidentalis*).
- Yew (*Taxus* spp.).

Boxwood

A boxwood hedge can live for several hundred years, and you can shear it into a tight form or leave it to grow in a more natural, bushy shape. Choose a variety suitable for your climate because some varieties can turn brown in colder climates. Boxwood is one of the slower-growing hedge plants, growing only a few inches each year. It is more shade tolerant than some other evergreen shrubs. But, boxwood emits a strong ammonia smell certain times of the year so think about planting them away from entryways and windows.

Privet

Privet is used as a hedge throughout the United States. It grows so well that it is discouraged in some parts of the

United States because of its ability to spread far and wide with the help of seed-eating birds. Privet is an easy-to-grow hedge because it has a complicated root system consisting of shallow surface roots and a deep **taproot**, which is the central main root that reaches deep into the ground and has other roots growing off it; such a root system makes it drought tolerant once established. It can recover quickly from the most severe pruning because it grows fast and can reach heights of 4 to 15 feet so you do not need to worry if your shearing job is a little off: You will have the chance to correct it in a few weeks. If your privet gets out of hand or if you moved into a home with large unsightly privet, cut it back to 6 inches from the ground; it will come back as a healthy, multi-branched shrub.

Holly

Holly is a good shrub for a hedge if you use a variety that grows well in your area because some varieties are not cold hardy. The American holly (*Ilex opaca*) has the classic thorny leaves you think of when you think of hollies, but some varieties like yaupon holly (*Ilex vomitoria*) have smooth leaves. All hollies will recover after they are drastically cut back, sending out numerous new shoots by the next season. The best way to manage a holly hedge is to start pruning early in the life of the plant so new growth fills in and creates a thick, beautiful hedge. To create an interesting and different hedge, you can prune a yaupon holly in a way that you remove all lower lateral limbs from the bottom two-thirds of the trunk, leaving only the most attractive multiple bare trunks. Leave the top third of the hedge covered in vegetation. Then, cut the top growth back to the desired height to create a bonsai-style hedge. There is a weeping variety of yaupon holly available, but its crooked trunk and curved branches make it more suitable as a corner plant.

All hollies have the potential to produce the classic red berries, but only the Chinese hollies, such as the Burford holly (*Ilex cornuta*), produce berries on female plants without a male pollinator. All other varieties need a male pollinator planted close by for the female plants to produce berries. Of course, this is not a problem if you plant the shrubs in a row. Unfortunately, there is not an easy way to tell if a holly plant is male or female so you can expect some hollies in a hedgerow to not have berries, unless they are a variety of Chinese holly.

Canadian hemlock

Canadian hemlock and Carolina hemlock (*Tsuga caroliniana*) can be sheared in late spring or early summer and provide a hedge with graceful, feathery foliage. Hemlock grows slower than most hedges but lasts a long time. The limbs thickly grow from the ground up. Because the natural form is a tree, the plant needs proper shearing to maintain its shape. It will spread out as far as 30 feet and become unruly if not sheared regularly. Hemlocks can tolerate shade more than other shrubs used as hedges.

The native habitat of hemlocks is cool and moist so you should not grow them in USDA Horticultural Zones 8 and warmer. Because of the potential to grow large, you should not plant hemlocks close to a house.

American arborvitae

The American arborvitae grows slowly when young, but growth speeds up when it is around 4 or 5 years old. They are one of the few conifers that break green growth from woody stems after a severe shearing so they can handle extensive pruning even though they need little care. The best times to prune your arborvitae are in fall and early winter. If pruned in summer, their branch tips tend to brown. Arborvitae do best in full sun or partial shade, and they do well in cold climate and moist soil. Hot, dry soil will cause your arborvitae to suffer. You should put a protective net or burlap over them in winter — snow and ice can damage and break their branches. Netting is actually the better choice because mold and mildew can grow under burlap. Because of their multiple trunks and limbs and how terrible they initially look after sheared back, most people do not know what to do with arborvitae and simply have them removed from the landscape when they become too large. Although you may feel your arborvitae is too close to your house, you can manage these hedges effectively. The best way to handle an overgrown arborvitae is to grab your shears, take a deep breath, and dive in. If planted for a hedge, plant three arborvitae 5 feet apart for dense coverage. An arborvitae hedge can be attractive if all you do is simply shear off the top at the desired height once a year. In addition, you do not necessarily have to create an arborvitae hedge in order to get a hedge-like feel. Many gardeners plant arborvitae side by side, about 5 feet apart, and then let them grow naturally, with occasional pruning of dead branches. Over time, the arborvitae will grow into each other, creating a tall, naturally formed hedge.

Yews

Yews have thin evergreen leaves that grow thickly and make a dense hedge. There is a yew for every landscape because you have many different varieties to choose from. Yews are classified as medium-fast growers, and some types only grow a few feet tall so they may never need shearing. You can cut back yews hard, and they will sprout new growth from old wood. **Foundation planting**, or planting close to a structure that sits on a cement foundation, is not recommended because of the large and woody root system of a yew.

Barrier hedges

You can use hedges for barriers to prevent pedestrian traffic or to make you feel more secure. The best hedges for barriers are shrubs with thorny branches. Keep in mind that having thorny barrier plants in a place where someone could get injured without crossing your property could result in a personal injury lawsuit. If you have a homeowners association where you live, you should also check to see if you can have barrier hedges before you plant. Good choices for a thorny or barrier hedge include:

- Barberry (*Berberis atropurpurea*).
- Hawthorn (*Crataegus monogyna*).
- Crabapple (*Malus sylvestris*).
- Shrub roses (*Rosa rugosa*).

Barberry

Barberry grows 4 to 5 feet tall and has bright red foliage and vicious thorns that make it a good barrier hedge. In the fall, it produces bright red berries that attract a variety of songbirds. You should plant it 2 to 4 feet apart to create a solid, impenetrable hedge. Barberry grows well in USDA Horticultural Zones 4 through 8, but it will suffer fungal problems in warm, humid climates.

Hawthorn

Hawthorn, or European Hawthorn, grows wildly throughout North America, but it is also cultivated. The hawthorn has long and stiff thorns. It is one of the few plants still used as a livestock barrier. It produces a profusion of white or pink flowers that look similar to berry blossoms. After the flowers die, a red fruit, called a **haw**, grows. The haw is about the size of a crabapple, and you can leave it on the plant for wildlife to eat, or you can use it to make jellies and jams. You can shear hawthorn bushes into a tight hedge.

There are several varieties available that grow to different sizes and have varying degrees of thorniness so choose one appropriate for your landscape. Hedgelaying is often done with the hawthorn.

Crabapple

Crabapple varieties are shrubs or small trees that can grow up to 50 feet tall. They create a point of interest in the spring when they bloom pink, white, or red flowers and in the fall when they lose their leaves and only the red crabapples remain. A wide range of wildlife and birds eat crabapples, and people harvest the fruit for jams and jellies. For use as a flowering hedge, prune right after blooming for better bloom production the next year. For the best flowering results, choose varieties growing on their own roots rather than grafted varieties. The fruit may not be as large, but they make a better hedge with a longer life, less suckering, and more disease resistance. If you want maximum fruit production for the next year, delay pruning until after the fruit matures in winter or early spring if you want maximum fruit production for that year. Late fall and winter are good times to rake up old fruit on the ground that could spread fungal diseases to the plants.

Shrub roses

Shrub roses are suitable for planting 2 feet apart in average, well-drained garden soil. The blooms are single, daisy-like blossoms, not like florist roses with multiple petals.

Although they have plenty of thorns and can reach heights to 6 feet or higher, their most interesting feature is the large and colorful rose hips or seed pods that appear after the blooms fade. Shrub roses grow best in USDA Horticultural Zones 2 through 8. Like the barberry, they will suffer from mildew problems in areas with high humidity. You can shear them after blooming, but this means you will remove the rose hips. Shrub roses grow up to 10 feet tall.

Creating a Hedge

Modern hedges are a group of bushes usually planted and maintained in a long row. The first thing to do when planning a hedge is to find the right shrub for the job so you should figure out what height you want your hedge. Think about what areas the hedge will shade, such as your neighbor's yard or a vegetable garden. Check to see if the sight line of someone driving by or your sight line backing out of the driveway will be blocked. Do the research to find out what bushes are right for your climate and planting zone by contacting your local county extension office for suggestions for the right bush to plant as a hedge or by researching it on the Internet. If a neighbor's yard has a hedge you like, ask your neighbor about it, and inquire about how to maintain the plant. Be careful when shopping in a catalogue or actually buying on the Internet when it comes to purchasing plants. A shrub or tree is likely a long-term addition to your landscape, and a bad purchase decision can be costly in terms of the initial cost and eventual removal if the plant turns out to be the wrong choice or is of poor quality. Buy your shrubs and prepare to plant them in early spring in areas where the ground freezes in winter. If you live in a climate where it does not freeze in the winter, purchase shrubs in the fall.

Measure the area to find the exact length of your new hedge and how many plants you will need for fast coverage. A good rule of thumb is to plant a bush every 2 feet for a nice thick hedge. If you order the shrubs and they come by mail, they are probably **bare root**, which means the roots have no soil around them, so immediately soak the plants in a bucket of warm water while you prepare the planting area. If you cannot plant the bare root plants in less than 24 hours after receiving them, you need to dig a trench, lay the root sections in the trench, and cover them with damp soil until you are ready to plant. This is called "heeling in" the plant. Soaking some bare root plants for more than 24 hours can drown them by cutting off oxygen to their roots. If you are buying container plants, be sure they stay in a sheltered area and receive water every day until planted.

Mark off the area you will plant your hedges by hammering two stakes in the ground at each end of the proposed hedgerow, and draw a string between them. Because the plants are planted so close together, it might be easier to dig a trench to plant them in rather than digging a series of smaller holes. After you dig the trench, add your new plants 2 feet apart. Run water around the roots while you backfill with the same soil removed from the hole. If you have chosen the right shrub for your area, you do not need to add any amendments to the soil other than a little compost. If you are adding **drip irrigation** — also known as trickle irrigation, where water is allowed to drip slowly onto the roots of plants through a drip hose or valve — put it down after filling the area around the new plants. Then, cover the irrigation line, as well as the root zone of the new plants, with a 1-inch layer of mulch.

Pruning must begin as soon as you plant the shrubs. If the plants already have lateral branches extending out at ground level, then cut a third off the top of the shortest plant in the group. Then, cut all the other plants to the same height as the one you just cut. Do not prune again until the following season. If the plants are spindly with only top growth, cut them all down to 3 to 4 inches from the ground. This will encourage basal branching. Remember that a hedge only looks good if the branches extend from the base of the plant to the top. Early in the second spring, cut all the plants back halfway. From the third year on, shape by cutting back half all new growth, keeping in mind that the bottom should be wider than the top. Repeat as needed to keep your hedge in shape until you achieve the final height. Once you obtain your desired height, prune as needed. Remember that flowering shrubs are pruned as soon after the bloom period as possible so you do not damage blooms developing for the next season. If the shrubs bloom more than once during the season, such as some roses and azaleas, prune as needed right after each bloom period.

Keep the planting area free of weeds for as long as possible. Eventually, the hedges will shade out any weed competition.

This man is pruning the hedge in his backyard to give it a neat appearance.

If you have chosen plants appropriate for your area, minimal fertilization will be required, but be sure the plants receive adequate moisture until they are established, which is after at least one growing season. If one shrub dies in the hedgerow, replace it as soon as possible. If you wait too long, the roots from the remaining shrubs will grow into the space of the dead plant used. It is easier to replace the plant quickly rather than to spend time cutting and damaging roots from the neighboring shrubs.

Up to this point, the discussion on hedges has centered on the formal shearing of hedges and creating clean, formal lines. With certain landscapes or plant varieties, a more natural look is needed, especially with shrubs that bloom on long canes or new shoots, such as spirea, nandina, or lady banksia rose. In these situations, shearing will ruin the overall shape of the plant and destroy the bloom or berry production. To keep the natural shape of a shrub but decrease the size, locate the largest unruly cane that needs taming. Follow the unruly cane down to a main branch or to the ground, and cut there. This is called a **heading cut**. When cutting the unruly cane from a main branch, remember to cut at the main branch without leaving a stub. A rotting stub left on the plant creates a favorable environment for disease. Take a few steps back, and carefully choose the next cane to remove. Repeat until the plant reaches the desired height and size. The procedure may seem tedious and time consuming, but the plant will look better and more natural when you finish.

Hedge mazes, such as this, developed from the English knot garden.

An old, overgrown hedge

If you find yourself looking at a row of privet or other hedge plant that has not seen a pruning shear in ten years or more, you may wonder what to do to make it look good again. Your approach depends on how much growth is growing near the bottom of the hedgerow.

- If the bottom of the hedgerow has no green growth at the bottom, cut the entire row down to 4 to 5 inches from the ground, and start pruning as if you had a new plant.

- If the hedge looks salvageable, cut out the dead limbs with a saw or loppers. Try to cut the dead limbs back to a live branch or the ground. Next, stand back and look at the largest limbs reaching skyward, and cut them back to the base of the plant where they join a main limb or emerge from the ground. Now, you should only have the smaller unruly growth. Cut it all back to a level half of the eventual height of the hedgerow. As it grows, continue to cut off half the new growth until you obtain the desired size. It should grow in thickly and create a nice hedge. Remember the ideal shape for the hedge is a little wider at the bottom so lower limbs get some light and remain full and green.

A hedge for wildlife

A group of shrubs provides a natural shelter for wildlife, and the larger the group of shrubs, the more wildlife protection it provides. Any hedge can provide protection for small animals just because it provides shelter from wind and rain, but if you want to attract more wildlife to your hedge, you simply need to make a few changes in the design. Although attracting wildlife may not be the best choice for everyone, it can add some fun to your landscape.

Wildlife likes a diversity of plants in a hedge that provides shelter and food throughout the year. Keep in mind that wildlife is not concerned about how neat, sheared, and uniform your hedges look to the neighbors. If you live in an area where you can get away with it, think about diversifying and letting your shrubs get a little unruly. Do some research and find out what native shrubs and small trees are browsed by wildlife most often in your area. For example, dogwood and American beautyberry are popular wildlife plants in the southeastern United States. Both of these plants attract various types of birds and animals because of their berries. Take note of the different sizes of shrubs and whether they thrive in sun or shade and what type of wildlife they attract. Find out what wild berry plants and native vines grow in your climate, and finally, look for a recommended wildflower mix. Try to find a wildflower mix containing some native grasses, along with the wildflower seed. Birds and small mammals eat native grass seeds, and birds use the leaves for nest building.

A wildlife hedge needs a wider space than a conventional hedge because of the diversity it provides. The ground does not need any special preparation except the removal of existing grass and weeds. Plant the small trees first, about 10 feet apart, and inter-plant shrubs that grow slightly smaller. On the sides of the larger shrubs, plant lower-growing blooming perennials so you can see the butterflies and hummingbirds during the summer. Lastly, plant a few berry vines around the entire hedgerow, topping off everything by scattering wildflower and native grass seed around the outer perimeter. If you have an old wooden fence to act as the center of your wildlife hedge, you are lucky because it adds interest and support to the entire planting. Long stretches of barbwire fence normally kept clear of vegetation make a great place to start a wildlife hedge. Although it sounds like you will create an eyesore by planting in layers, you and the wildlife receive great rewards. You are rewarded with the beauty of the layered hedges, as well as the wildlife they attract, and wildlife is rewarded with possible food and habitat. Be sure to use native plants because non-native plants, such as privet, grow quickly and overwhelm the wildlife hedge in a few years. The same goes for choosing vines; choose native and noninvasive vines, such as trumpet vine or cross vine. You can use a much smaller variation of this wildlife hedge design if you live in a suburb by dedicating a corner of your yard for wildlife. If you only have a patio, plant a combination of native plants in containers close together to attract wildlife. Add to the attraction by putting up a bird feeder or two. In a big city, it can be a welcome sight to look on your patio and see colorful hummingbirds or butterflies.

Chapter 12:

Pruning Evergreens

Evergreen trees are popular, especially in northern climates where deciduous trees lose their leaves. They provide color to counter the winter bareness of deciduous plants and make a great focal point in your garden. Many evergreen trees are conifers — that is, they bear cones. But, just as many types of evergreens produce berries instead.

Most evergreens need little pruning if you allow yours to grow naturally. If you decide to conform your plant to a specific shape or size, then expect to spend more time pruning it than usual. In this situation, you may want to pick an evergreen that will mature close to the size you desire. Although evergreens make up a broad list of plants, most do not need special pruning at planting, nor do most react with shock when transplanted.

You can distinguish conifers from berried evergreens by the cones they produce, although sometimes those cones look like seeds, as in the case of yews. They also have needled leaves, as opposed to broadleaf evergreens that produce berries instead of cones. Some popular conifers include pines, spruces, firs, yews, arborvitae, cypress, hemlock, and juniper, whereas familiar broadleaf evergreens make up an extensive list that include azalea, holly, mountain laurel, rhododendron, bougainvillea, jasmine, gardenia, oleander, camellia, hibiscus, and olive.

General Rules About Pruning Needled Evergreens

The challenge with pruning needled evergreens is they have a fast growing season that occurs for only three weeks, although there are a few, such as the hemlocks and junipers, that have a longer growing period, while the yew also grows in summer. This short opportunity is the perfect time to prune your needled evergreens. This growing period includes pines, most spruces, firs, and yews, and it happens around April in warmer climates and mid-June in colder areas. Arborvitae, cypress, hemlock, and juniper start their growing periods a little later.

Follow these four basic principles when pruning needled evergreens:

1. First, start when the tree or bush is small. If you wait until your plant reaches the height you desire, you will have a harder time getting the shape you want so begin shearing when it is young.

2. Only prune off a third of your tree or bush. More than that at one time will result in shock.

3. Shear your evergreen every year. If you miss one year's pruning, you will have a difficult time shaping your tree or bush again.

4. Shear when new growth is wet, such as in the early morning or after rain.

Shearing a needled evergreen tree or bush ensures a bushier plant. Shearing once a year will give your plant a natural look, but this can cause the tree to grow too large. If your goal is to confine your plant to a certain space or shape, you may need to shear it two or three times each year. You can prune lightly and let your tree or shrub grow gradually, or you can prune severely so your plant stays small but thicker.

When shearing needled evergreens, you should stick to the shape you desire it to be when it reaches the height you want it to be. Remove terminal buds, the fat brown buds at the end of each twig that form the previous year, and dormant buds, which are thousands of almost invisible smaller buds on the twigs and branches. Dormant buds do not grow, but if you shear them during the evergreen's growth period, it will stop the active growth of the terminal buds and stimulate the sprouting and growth of the dormant buds.

Also, be aware of the two different growth patterns of needled conifers: random branching and whorled branching. It is important to realize the difference so you prune your specific plant accordingly.

Conifers with random branching have branches that sprout anywhere along the trunk and branches. These type of needled evergreens grow in spurts through the growing season, and they also vary in their ability to re-sprout if cut back into older wood. Shearing will make growth denser, but how much to shear will depend on whether your particular tree or bush sprouts from both old wood and new wood or just from new wood alone. Also, random branching conifers handle pruning well because their bud locations and growth timing are not rigidly programmed as in the whorled branching conifers. You can train a random branching tree by cutting back wayward branches or removing them completely to promote denser growth. If you desire to limit the size of your random branching evergreen, shorten branches before growth begins each season.

Conifers with whorled branching have branches growing in whorls at intervals along the trunk or stems, with few latent buds or dormant growing points on the leafless parts of the branch. These branches will not re-grow if cut back. On whorled branching conifers, each bud is programmed for all the growth it will do for that season so if you want to make a whorled branching evergreen bushier or if you want to slow its growth, you need to pinch back new growth in the spring when the buds expand but before they fully expand. If you want to remove branches altogether, prune just before growth begins so new growth will hide these cuts.

Needled evergreens often grow into a naturally spire-like shape, but you will need to prune to train it into a single central leader when young. With conifers, there is rarely competition with the central leader, but should there be, cut those shoots off completely to avoid having more than one shoot developing into leaders. This will prevent upsetting the symmetry of the tree and will also prevent old, dead bark from building up in the narrow crotch between the leaders that will not have living tissue to join them and possibly cause a split between the leaders as the tree ages.

Sometimes a leader can sustain damage or break off. If your conifer is a whorled branching tree, one or more of the top branches may then bend upward and try to become the leader. You will have to choose which branch will be the leader and stake it to the remaining portion of the damaged leader. This will cause the other branches competing for leadership to droop back to their previous positions. If a bud develops on the damaged leader, it may grow an upright shoot. Choose this as the leader over any top branch because it will be more vigorous and in a better position to serve as leader of your tree.

Whether your needled conifer is a random branching or whorled branching variety, it will require minimal pruning once trained and shaped. Watch out for overcrowded limbs because you run the risk of some branches not receiving adequate light and possibly dying with overcrowding. Thin out overcrowded laterals and also remove any dead or diseased wood. In addition, be aware that lower branches may die as the tree or shrub ages so remove these branches slowly over the years rather than risk shocking your plant.

If you are attempting to shear your conifer into a specific shape, keep in mind that this requires a lot of work. Over time, as you cut back branch tips while leaving a little of the earlier growth, your sheared evergreen will grow larger and larger, eventually outgrowing its space. Also, avoid severe pruning because conifers rarely re-grow when extensively cut back. A better alternative to shaping a conifer is to choose one that is the right size and shape to begin with.

Popular Needle-leafed Evergreens

If your evergreen has needled leaves, then it is more likely in the pine, fir, cypress, or spruce family. Some of these trees have clusters or bundles of two to five needles, while others have single needles attached to their branches. Clustered needles include the various pines, while single-needled evergreens include the spruces, firs, cypress, yew, and hemlocks. Most needle-leaf trees are conifers.

Pines

Pines are needled conifers with whorled branching. There are 115 species of pine, and with a few exceptions — such as the Australian pine, red pine, and Scotch pine — most have no latent buds or dormant growing points. You can make your pine smaller by cutting main branches back to secondary branches when the pine is dormant. Another way to retain your pine's size is by pruning its candles. This will also make your tree fuller and bushier.

You can trick a mature pine into growing side branches if needed by cutting away a ring of bark about $\frac{1}{8}$ of a inch wide around the stem where you want the side branches to grow. Another trick is to remove needles about 1 to 2 inches beyond where you want branching to occur. Although these tactics work on a mature pine, they work best on younger pines. They also are most successful when you cut bark or remove needles close to the end of the stem.

Spruces

There are 35 varieties of spruce, and they all have whorled branching with few dormant buds. Spruces rarely need pruning because they have a naturally pleasing shape. When planting a young spruce, make sure you choose a dominant leader and remove any competing leaders. If you want to make your spruce smaller as it matures — they can grow from 66 to 200 feet high

— you need to prune back to the side branches or to the visible dormant buds. If you wish to make your plant denser or thicker, pinch lateral shoots when they are half-grown in the spring. You can also shear your tree right before growth starts and then shear again in late spring or early summer. Always wear thick protective gloves because the spruce's needles are quite prickly. Other than that, spruces need minimal pruning. Do not be tempted to prune lower branches — spruces look their best when their lower branches sweep the ground.

Firs

There are around 55 species of firs that can reach 30 to 260 feet tall. Firs have a whorled branching pattern, few dormant buds, and a short space between needles along the stem. They are naturally dense conifers and need minimal pruning. Should you desire a denser fir, simply pinch developing shoots in the spring, and cut branches growing in odd directions back to the laterals. Do not pinch the top whorl, unless trying to restrict your fir's height because the top whorl will not re-grow, or if it does, it will do so poorly.

Yews

The yew is a popular flat-needled evergreen found in many gardens because of its attractive yellow color. Yews have random branching patterns and seldom need pruning.  Their branches have dormant growing points, and because of this, the yew can handle severe pruning if necessary — for example, if it has overgrown — and it will rebound with gusto. For example, if you want to control the size and shape of your plant, make heading and thinning cuts back to old wood. You can also make this conifer denser by pruning the end of its stems by a third to a half. You can grow it as a bush or train it as a tree. If you are shaping it again, cut stems back by a third to a half. Also, if you live in a cold climate, round the tops because yews tend to grow flat tops that can catch snow that can damage its branches. Trim the new overlong shoots that often sprout up and out after winter pruning. Make sure you do your pruning gradually, a little at a time each winter. In three years, you should have the yew in the size and shape you desire.

Arborvitae

The arborvitae is another type of random branching conifer that can grow upward of 40 feet tall. They are easy to care for and can handle severe pruning, although they actually require little maintenance. It is best to prune them annually to keep them under control because they are fast-growing conifers. The best time to prune your arborvitae is in the late fall or early winter. You can  prune an arborvitae in spring or summer, but their tips tend to brown when pruned in warmer weather.

Prune the wood back to side branches or where there is foliage, or make the tree denser by cutting back the tops of the stems. Arborvitaes tend to naturally grow in a cone shape, but if you want to shape your tree even more, it can withstand extensive shearing. But, the best shape to prune your arborvitae is a rounded or pointed top because this is its natural growing pattern. Make sure the base is wider than the top so sunlight can reach the lower branches.

Cypress

Cypresses are fast-growing, random-branching conifers that need minimal pruning. A cypress can grow 3 to 4 feet a year, up to 70 feet tall and up to 20 feet wide. Should you decide to prune yours, it can sprout new growth wherever it has leaves. Make sure you do so in dry weather because wet weather will introduce it to disease. If you are shaping your cypress — which is seldom necessary — cut branches back to either a lateral or to a point where there are leaves. To make your tree denser, prune back the tips of the branches. Also, remove any dead or diseased branches by cutting the stem back to where it is healthy. If your cypress is getting too tall, cut off the top, and if it is too wide, shape it by cutting back its side branches. Cypress can get quite dense so you may want to thin branches on the inside of the tree so sunlight and air circulation can reach the center. Keep in mind that cypresses grow slowly after pruning.

Hemlock

Hemlocks are naturally full and can be grown as trees or bushes. If grown as trees, they can reach up to 60 to 80 feet tall and 25 to 30 feet wide. But, they grow slowly and tightly, which is why they are often used as windbreaks or privacy screens. They have a random branching pattern and a natural cone-shaped form, and they can re-sprout stems from bare wood. To prune or shape your hemlock tree, do it in late winter so you make your cuts before new growth begins. Do it over a series of a few years so less stress on the tree occurs. If your hemlock needs rejuvenation, severe pruning works best.

Juniper

Junipers are in the cypress family and have random branching with growing points even where there are no leaves. They also produce berries. Junipers have a naturally attractive form and need minimal pruning,

but they can withstand the most severe pruning more than any other kind, with leaves that are either needles or scales, depending on the species. The scale-like leaf species can withstand more severe pruning than the needle type, but both endure major shearing.

You can prune your juniper tree or bush at any time of the year, except summer. If you want a denser juniper, cut back the stem tips. To remove larger branches, shorten them to the weaker laterals. This will make your juniper plant smaller but will open up the interior to light and air. This helps because interior branches on junipers often die out because of the thickness of the plant that causes intense shading in the center of the tree. Also, remove any stems or branches sticking out from the rest of the plant. Although junipers can handle intense pruning, never cut beyond the green part of a branch. If you do, your branch will not grow back.

General Rules About Pruning Broadleaf Evergreens

Broadleaf evergreens are the opposite of needled evergreens in that they need little pruning as they mature. What pruning they do need is similar among this very extensive list. In general, the rules of thumb are as follows:

1. Train when young with early pruning in order to create or encourage your broadleaf's natural shape.

2. Shape your tree or shrub in early summer, after your plant has finished blooming and is actively growing. Do this by snipping off the terminal or end buds on new sprouts in order to force latent buds to develop and grow along the branches. To keep your bush

small, pinch off terminal buds for the remainder of your shrub's life.

3. Do not remove the large, fat buds because they are next year's blossoms.

4. Most broadleaf evergreens need rejuvenation or renovation from time to time, spread out over two or more years. Do this in late winter or early spring. This includes shortening long branches, removing dead or damaged branches, thinning out thick growth, and cutting back the remaining branches.

Early pruning is a necessity in order to train broadleaf evergreens, but only prune a little so you can bring out the plant's natural shape. When your plant is young, allow one vertical shoot to be the central leader, unless you are creating a bush. This central leader will become the trunk. Remove any other stems competing for leadership position. Branches growing off this central leader will eventually become the main scaffolding branches of your tree. Choose these main branches when your tree is young, and make sure they are spaced far enough apart — between 6 to 18 inches — so they will not become overcrowded as your tree matures. Allow some temporary branches to also grow off the trunk in order to strengthen your tree, but prune them back once they start getting big. Also, choose side branches growing off your scaffolding branches that are not growing closely, and prune off the rest.

If you are growing your broadleaf as a bush, however, allow multiple stems to grow from the ground level. Then, select two or three as your main trunks, cut off the branches growing from these trunks, and cut the other stems back to the ground.

If you want your broadleaf smaller, prune just before growth begins, cutting back the side branches within the tree or bush. You may want to wait until the plant has flowered in order to enjoy the beautiful blooms. But, if you want your tree or bush to grow denser, prune the plant when it is dormant in winter, or pinch new shoots when they actively grow in early summer. Snip off the terminal or end bud of new sprouts. This will force latent buds to grow along the sides of the branches. Once your broadleaf plant starts blooming, pinch off the small end buds of any branches growing too long, but leave the bigger, fat blossom buds because these will bloom the following year. If your broadleaf is a bush and you want it to stay compact, you will need to do this kind of pruning for its entire life.

When needed, you can remove a stem growing in the wrong direction by cutting it off at its point of origin or back to one of its side branches. Your broadleaf tree or bush will not need much pruning as it matures, but always remove dead or diseased wood and branches that cross or rub against each other.

Azalea

The azalea is a broadleaf evergreen in the rhododendron family that blooms every spring and summer and is stocked with leaves and growth buds along its stems. Azaleas need periodic pruning in order to shape them, to remove dead or diseased wood that sometimes occurs in winter, or to remove suckers growing from the base. You want to prune your azalea bush as soon as it blooms.

If you want to shape your azalea plant — or renew one that needs rejuvenation — shorten or remove the stems back to where there is green wood, unless you are removing larger branches, which you should cut off flush with the trunk. Pinch the growing tips once or twice up until August to cause your plant to become bushier and encourage branching because azaleas can sometimes become leggy or bare near the bottom. Also, remove any dead or overgrown wood in the center of the plant to allow the bush to receive more sunlight and air circulation in the center.

With the exception of pinching the growing tips, stop all pruning by June if you desire early blooms for the following year because azalea flower buds take eight to ten weeks to develop in warm weather. If your azalea shrub has become overgrown for its space in your garden, prune it back to about 1 foot tall.

Holly

Hollies come in many varieties and need pruning annually. Your tree or bush requires pruning in December when the plant is dormant. Prune carefully and only as needed for

health, structure, and form, but do not prune severely or cut back into the leafless portions if you desire re-growth. Pruning for a specific shape is not suggested. Hollies do best when allowed to grow in their natural form.

Start from the inside of your tree or shrub and work your way outward. Remove dead or diseased branches, as well as rubbing or crossing branches and long and spindly branches. When trimming branches, cut just above new leaf buds or all the way back to the main branch. This will cause the plant to fill in with new growth, creating a bushier tree or bush the following year.

Mountain laurel

Mountain laurel is a broadleaf that can grow up to 12 feet tall. It needs little pruning beyond for shaping and for health, such as removing dead or diseased wood. The best time to prune mountain laurel is right after its flowers fade in May or June. This will cause your shrub to direct its energy into producing more blooms the following year. If you want to promote growth, such as when cutting back a leggy branch or if you need to renovate a bush doing poorly or becoming overgrown, cut the branches back to the root. Keep in mind that mountain laurels do best with a light touch.

Rhododendron

Rhododendrons are broad-leafs that need little pruning beyond shaping or renovating. They tend to be leggy, but you can encourage new branches by pinching off terminal buds just before they grow and also by pinching any growing shoots before their leaves expand. Terminal growth buds are slender, whereas flower buds are fat and stubby. The best time to prune a rhododendron is

right after it flowers. If your plant outgrows its space in your garden, cut it back drastically after it finishes flowering. Drastically in this case means a few branches a year — since rhododendrons do not always grow new growth from old stems — until the plant reaches your desired size. Once you have pruned it, choose new main stems from the shoots that do grow as a result of the pruning. Do not expect to see new blooms for the next year or two.

Bougainvillea

Bougainvilleas are broadleaf evergreens that can be grown as shrubs or vines. The best time to prune them is in summer or early fall. Bougainvilleas can take severe pruning, but be careful — they have sharp thorns along the stems. If you have limited space in your garden, choose two or three main stems, and cut back the rest. Also, shorten any thin stems just before growth begins. If you want to encourage blooming, pinch off the tips of the stems. This will also cause the plant to grow fuller and branch out more evenly. Do not forget to thin out the center of any dead or diseased branches or branches that rub against each other. This will create more opportunity for sunlight to reach the center of the plant. You can also turn your bougainvillea into a non-clinging vine by growing it from one or two stems.

Jasmine

Jasmine can do fine without pruning, but cutting it back on a regular basis will promote more growth of its intensely fragrant blooms. Jasmine flowers on year-old growth so you want to prune after it has flowered in the spring. If you pinch back the tips,

you will encourage lateral growth and more blooms for the following year. Remove suckers at the base so your plant will grow wider, and cut back stems about a third of the way to promote new growth. Cut back any scraggly stems, as well as dead or diseased wood, back to new wood just before a growing bud, and thin out overcrowded wood in the center to allow more air and sunlight to penetrate there. If you want your jasmine to thicken, pinch the growing tips to encourage branching.

Gardenia

Like many broadleaf evergreens, gardenia needs little pruning, except to shape or improve the health of the plant. The main reasons to prune your gardenia shrub is to remove any dead or diseased wood and to maintain the right size and shape for your garden. The best time to shorten stems and thin out twiggy branches is just before growth begins on the plant in late summer. If you want a denser shrub, promote further branching by pinching the tips of growing shoots — but do this by August at the latest. If your shrub needs rejuvenation, cut stems back severely because they will re-grow. The great and easy thing about a gardenia plant is that it can sprout growth on both new and old wood.

Oleander

Oleander is a large bush that sprouts freely from its base. The most important rule about pruning an oleander is to wear gloves and protective clothing because oleanders are highly poisonous. Having said that, it is an easy plant to prune. The best time for pruning is in September or October before new growth begins. Begin by pruning

just above a leaf node where three leaves come out of a branch. This will encourage new branching. But, if you want to control the size of your oleander, cut the oldest wood to ground level, and shorten any overly long stems to the side branches. If you want to make your shrub denser, pinch the shoot tips. If your oleander needs renovating or has been neglected, cut it to the ground so it will send up new shoots. You can also train an oleander to be a small tree. Do this by removing the lower branches and root suckers.

Camellia

The most pruning a camellia needs is just a little to shape your plant and maintain its health. If your shrub is young, thin the flower buds in order to direct energy into growth. On older camellias, you can thin flower buds to increase the size of the remaining blooms. Do your pruning after the plant's flowers have faded in May or June. The one thing about camellia is that its growth pattern can vary, from being too spread out when young to too gangly when older. Cut back the side branches to channel energy into vertical growth if the width of your plant is the problem, or head off some stems to the bases of the previous year's growth to encourage branching if you need to thicken your bush. You can also create a bushier plant by pinching the growing tips. If your camellia needs rejuvenation, cut the bush back to bare stems, but do it slowly over several seasons, or your plant may not re-grow.

Hibiscus

Hibiscus is a broadleaf that does not take well to shearing so if you are shaping it, prune selected branches instead.

It flowers on new growth, which you can stimulate by shortening stems by a third before new growth begins. You can promote thickness in a young hibiscus shrub simply by pinching its growing tips. If your hibiscus overgrows or needs renovating, cut back the old stems to side branches lower down on the plant. This is best done during the growing season in spring, but do not prune after August, or you will encourage new growth that frost in fall or winter can damage. It is always a good idea to thin out any overcrowding in the middle of the shrub by cutting off any crossing and rubbing branches or dead and diseased branches.

Olive

Olive is a broadleaf that can be grown to an ancient age. It is the oldest fruit tree known to man, with some living more than 2,000 years. If left to its own devices, it will grow dense, sending up basal sprouts and turning it into a bush instead. If you are planting a young olive tree, prune it with an open center and three scaffold branches. Remove the remaining branches, any water sprouts on the trunk and branches, and suckers near the root base. Then, wait until

your plant is 3 years old before choosing strong secondary branches and removing the rest. Prune in summer, and at all times, avoid pruning severely.

Once your olive tree is mature, prune to keep it from growing too large and to allow enough sunlight to reach the center and encourage new fruiting wood to grow. If your tree becomes heavy with fruit, thin the branches out in late spring or early summer. This will encourage less but larger fruit the following year. If you have an old olive tree that needs renovating, cut back some of the larger branches and thin out the new shoots that will grow as a result. Never cut an olive tree's branches back to the trunk; always leave a stub instead. Do not neglect to prune off any dead or diseased wood or branches that cross or rub against each other. You should also remove branches growing in a downward direction.

Conclusion

By now, you should feel confident about easily tackling any pruning job, large or small. The first step is, of course, to purchase your basic pruning tools, as well as gloves, eye goggles, and leather boots. Then, before you begin each pruning job, review your particular plant's unique qualities, growing style, and needs, and become well versed in the individual pruning techniques for that tree or shrub. Knowledge is power.

Take a deep breath, and remind yourself that expertise will come with experience. If you take your time, use the correct tool or tools for the job, and step back to view your work in between cuttings, you will avoid any costly, damaging, or permanent mistakes. Along the way, use this book as a handy reference guide for each individual tree or shrub. By proceeding carefully and deliberately and by educating yourself about your plants and the different pruning styles and techniques, you will soon realize that pruning is not so much a mystery as it is an acquired skill.

Do not forget to have fun while you are at it, and remind yourself that pruning is essential and prolongs the lives of your trees and shrubs. It is a small investment in time and effort on your part, and your plants will be healthier and more attractive as a result. Before you know it, you will have that beautiful garden you envision.

Recognizing Hazardous Defects in Trees

—Information and Photos Courtesy of the USDA.

Introduction

Trees add to our enjoyment of outdoor experiences whether in forests, parks, or urban landscapes. Too often, people are unaware of the risks associated with defective trees, which can cause personal injury and

property damage. Interest in hazard tree management has increased in recent years because of safety and liability concerns resulting from preventable accidents. Recognizing hazardous trees and taking proper corrective actions can protect property and save lives.

A "hazard tree" is a tree with structural defects likely to cause failure of all or part of the tree, which could strike a "target." A target can be a vehicle, building, or a place where people gather, such as a park bench, picnic table, street, or backyard.

Because of the natural variability of trees, the severity of their defects, and the different sites upon which they grow, evaluating trees for hazardous defects can be a complex process. This publication presents guidelines, not absolute rules for recognizing and correcting hazardous defects. When in doubt, consult an arborist.

What to Look For

Hazardous defects are visible signs that the tree is failing. Arborists recognize seven main types of tree defects: dead wood, cracks, weak branch unions, decay, cankers, root problems, and poor tree architecture. A tree with defects is not hazardous unless some portion of it is within striking distance of a target.

Dead wood

Dead wood is "not negotiable" — you must immediately remove dead trees and large dead branches. Dead trees and branches are unpredictable and can break and fall at any time. Dead wood is often dry and brittle and cannot bend in the wind like a living tree or branch. Dead branches and tree tops that are already broken off — "hangers" or "widow makers" — are especially dangerous.

Take immediate action if...

- A broken branch or top is lodged in a tree.
- A tree is dead.
- A branch is dead and of sufficient size to cause injury — this will vary with height and size of branch.

Dead branches can break and fall at any time.

Cracks

A crack is a deep split through the bark, extending into the wood of the tree. Cracks are extremely dangerous because they indicate that the tree is already failing.

Take action if...

- A crack extends deeply into or completely through the stem.
- Two or more cracks occur in the same general area of the stem.
- A crack is in contact with another defect.
- A branch of sufficient size to cause injury is cracked.

A serious crack like this one indicates that the tree is already failing.

Weak branch unions are places where branches are not strongly attached to the tree. A weak union occurs when two or more similarly-sized, normally upright branches grow so close together that bark grows between the branches, inside the union. This ingrown bark does not have the structural strength of wood, and the union is much weaker than one that does not have included bark. The included

Weak branch unions.

bark may also act as a wedge and force the branch union to split apart. Trees with a tendency to form upright branches, such as elm and maple, often produce weak branch unions.

Weak branch unions also form after a tree or branch is tipped or topped when the main stem or a large branch is cut at a right angle to the direction of growth leaving a large branch stub. The stub inevitably decays, providing very poor support for new branches — "epicormic" branches — that develop along the cut branch.

Take action if...

- A weak branch union occurs on the main stem.
- A weak branch union is cracked.
- A weak branch union is associated with a crack, cavity, or other defect.

This weak branch union has failed, creating a highly hazardous situation.

Cankers

A canker is a localized area on the stem or branch of a tree, where the bark is sunken or missing. Wounding or disease cause cankers. The presence of a canker increases the chance of the stem breaking near the canker. A tree with a canker that encompasses more than half of the tree's circumference may be hazardous even if exposed wood appears sound.

Take action if...

- A canker or multiple cankers affect more than half of the tree's circumference.

- A canker is physically connected to a crack, weak branch union, a cavity, or other defect.

The large canker on this tree has seriously weakened the stem.

Root problems

Trees with root problems may blow over in wind storms. They may even fall without warning in summer when burdened with the weight of the tree's leaves. There are many kinds of root problems to consider, including severing or paving-over roots; raising or lowering the soil grade near the tree; parking or driving vehicles over the roots; or extensive root decay.

Severing roots decreases support and increases the chance of failure or death of the tree.

Soil mounding, twig dieback, dead wood in the crown, and off-color or smaller than normal leaves are symptoms often associated with root problems. Because most defective roots are underground and out of sight, aboveground symptoms may serve as the best warning.

Take action if...

- A tree is leaning with recent root exposure, soil movement, or soil mounding near the base of the tree.

- More than half of the roots under the tree's crown have been cut or crushed. These trees are dangerous because they do not have adequate structural support from the root system.

- Advanced decay is present in the root flares or "buttress" roots.

The mound (arrow) at the base of this tree indicates that the tree has recently begun to lean and may soon fail.

Poor tree architecture

Poor architecture is a growth pattern that indicates weakness or structural imbalance. Trees with strange shapes are interesting to look at but may be structurally defective. Poor architecture often arises after many years of damage from storms, unusual growing conditions, improper pruning, topping, and other damage.

A leaning tree may be a hazard. Because not all leaning trees are dangerous, any leaning tree of concern should be examined by a professional arborist.

Take action if...

- A tree leans excessively.
- A large branch is out of proportion with the rest of the crown.

This tree is decayed and badly out of balance because of poor maintenance. It is dangerous, and extremely unattractive.

Multiple defects

The recognition of multiple defects in a tree is critical when evaluating the tree's potential to fail. Multiple defects that are touching or are close to one another should be carefully examined. If more than one defect occurs on the tree's main stem, you should assume the tree is extremely hazardous.

Glossary

Alternate: Alternating leaf placement as opposed to opposite leaf placement on a stem.

Annual: Plants that go through a complete life cycle, including germinating, growing, flowering, seeding, and dying, all within one growing season.

Auxin: Chemical compounds or hormones that promote growth in plants.

Axil: The upper angle of where a leafstalk joins a stem or branch.

Bark: The outermost layers of stems, branches, and trunks of trees and shrubs.

Bark ridge: A raised bump or fold of bark on the upper side of a branch where the branch joins the trunk.

Branch: A secondary or lateral shoot or stem growing off a major stem or limb.

Branch collar: A swollen ring of bark on the lower side of a branch that connects the branch to the trunk or parent branch.

Bonsai: An artistic form of growing a dwarf plant in a shallow pot or tray.

Broadleaf: Evergreen trees and shrubs that produce blossoms and fruit.

Bush: Also known as a *shrub*, a woody plant with several stems rising from the base and lacking a single trunk.

Cambium layer: Behind the *phloem*, a thin layer of active tissue that produces new *phloem* cells on one side and new *xylem* cells on the other.

Canopy: The leafy cover or crown formed by the upper branches of a tree.

Central leader: The central stem of a tree, which is a continuation of the trunk and from which scaffolding or main branches grow.

Conifer: An evergreen tree or shrub that bears cones and has needle-like leaves.

Coppicing: The act of cutting a tree or shrub down to the ground and allowing multiple stems to grow in place of a trunk.

Cork cambium: The layer of cells under the bark responsible for creating new bark.

Crown: The canopy of a tree, including the branches, leaves, and reproductive systems growing off the trunk, and also where the roots and stem meet at soil level.

Crown raising: Removing the bottom limbs of a tree or shrub to "raise the skirt" or crown in order to create space under the tree or shrub.

Crown thinning: The thinning of branches throughout the tree or shrub to allow more light and air to circulate the center of the plant.

Crown reduction: Thinning out the tree or shrub branches so the size of the plant reduces; also known as *drop-crotching*.

Deadheading: Removing flowers that have already bloomed from a plant in order to prevent seed formation so it will form more blooms the following year.

Debudding: Pinching off buds of a plant to create fewer but larger blooms the following year.

Deciduous: A tree or shrub that drops its leaves each year, normally in fall or winter.

Drop-crotching: See *crown reduction.*

Epicormic sprouting: Shoots that grow on the main stem, trunk, or branches.

Espalier: A plant trained to grow in a two-dimensional form, normally against a wall, fence, or trellis.

Ever-blooming: A flowering plant that blooms several times in one year.

Evergreen: A broadleaf or needle-leaf tree or shrub that keeps its leaves year round.

Grafting: Joining two or more plants so they will grow as one plant.

Hair roots: Smaller roots that grow from established plant roots.

Hard pruning: Cutting back a shrub's growth to the ground or leaving just stubs.

Heartwood: Dead tissue that, along with sapwood, is part of the innermost layer that trees and shrub depend on for support.

Hedge: A row of shrubs or low growing trees planted to form a fence or barrier.

Hedgelaying: The process of grafting a hedge to another hedge to form a barrier.

Knot garden: A formal garden made up of tightly sheared shrubs that, when viewed from above, appear to weave around each other, creating the appearance of a Celtic knot.

Lateral: The branches on the sides of a tree.

Leader: The main stem that grows from the trunk of a plant from which other branches grow.

Lion tails: Tufts of foliage and branches at the ends of main branches caused by removing all the inner lateral foliage and branches, which if not removed can cause sun scalding on the branches and trunk of a tree.

Modified central leader: The training of a young tree that combines a central leader form with an open center form.

Needle-leaf: Evergreen trees or shrubs that have leaves like needles.

New wood: Stems and branches that grow during the current growing season.

Node: The point where a leaf attaches to a stem.

Old wood: Stems and branches that grew during the previous year's growing season.

Open center: The training of a young tree to have a vase shape with three or four branches growing outward and upward from the trunk.

Ornamental: Plants that are either dwarf-sized trees, normally in pots, or pruned in a decorative fashion as part of a garden setting.

Phloem: The layer of cells behind the cambium layer on a trunk that conducts food from the leaves and moves it to the roots or other areas of the plant that need food.

Photosynthesis: The process of a plant using sunlight shining on the leaves to create a simple sugar to use as food and energy.

Pinching: Removing the tip of a growing shoot with your finger and thumb or fingernail.

Pleaching: Weaving branches of two or more trees together to form a living wall, roof, or tunnel.

Pollarding: Cutting off or stubbing back all the growth of a tree to the same point on a branch or trunk in order to sprout new growth during the growing season.

Pruning: The act of clearing vegetation from a plant to remove diseased tissue, stimulate growth, increase fruit or nut production, or control the space that a plant occupies.

Random branching: The growth pattern of a needled conifer where branches sprout up anywhere along the trunk and branches so the conifer grows in spurts during the growing season.

Renovation: To revitalize or renew an old or neglected plant.

Root crown: The transitional area at the surface of the soil where roots turn into woody stems as they grow from the ground.

Root graft: The thickened offset area at the base of a single tree trunk or bush where a type of root system with favorable characteristics is grafted to a plant with other desirable characteristics.

Root pruning: The cutting back of the roots of a plant in order to prepare a plant for transplanting, to slow the growth of a plant, to force blooms and fruit production, or to keep a container plant healthy.

Sapwood: Part of the *xylem* where water and nutrients flow upward to the top of the tree or shrub.

Scaffold branches: The major branches of a tree.

Shear: To do light pruning with various tools called shears to cut, clip, or remove small branches, stems, and water sprouts.

Shoot: An actively growing stem.

Shrub: Also known as a *bush*, a woody plant with several stems rising from the base and lacking a single trunk.

Standard: A tree or bush trained to have a clear trunk and a leafy or rounded bushy head.

Spur: A stubby flowering branch that grows slowly.

Suckers: Shoots that grow from the base of a tree or shrub.

Topiary: A tree or shrub pruned to create a shape or sculpture.

Transpiration: The process of excess water evaporating from pores on the underside of leaves.

Tree: A perennial woody plant that grows an average of 15 feet or more, marked by a distinct main trunk with branches growing out of the sides of the trunk.

Vine topiary: The process of allowing a vine to grow on top of a topiary tree or shrub.

Water sprout: A vigorously growing shoot that grows from a branch or trunk of a tree.

Whip: A young tree that consists of an unbranched single stem.

Whorls: An arrangement of three or more leaves or petals growing from a single node.

Whorled branching: Conifers that have branches growing in whorls at intervals along the trunk or stems with few latent buds or dominant growing points on the leafless parts of the branch.

Xylem: The entire inner part of the woody structure that is located behind the *cambium layer* and is the supporting and water-conducting tissue of the plant.

Bibliography

Brown, George E. *The Pruning of Trees, Shrubs and Conifers*. Portland, Oregon: Timber Press, Inc., 2004.

Creative Homeowner. *Smart Guide: Pruning*. Upper Saddle River, New Jersey: Federal Marketing Corporation, 2009.

Hicks, Ivan and Rosenfeld, Richard. *Tricks With Trees: Growing, Manipulating and Pruning*. London, United Kingdom: Pavilion Books, 2007.

Hill, Lewis. *Pruning Made Easy*. North Adams, Massachusetts: Storey Publishing, 1997.

Reich, Lee. "Standard Procedures." **www.oldhousejournal.com/standard_procedures/magazine/1414**.

Reich, Lee. *The Pruning Book*. Newtown, Connecticut: The Taunton Press, 1999.

American National Standards Institute. **www.ansi.org**.

"How to Prune Trees and Bushes."
**www.gardening-resources.co.uk/How_to_prune_
trees_and_bushes.php.**

"How to Make Your Own Topiary."
**www.gardeningknowhow.com/gardening-how-to/
how-to-make-your-own-topiary.htm**.

Author Biography

K.O. Morgan has more than 30 years of writing experience. She has been published in numerous magazines and written three books entitled *Living Smart: Healing Foods, Living Smart: Boosting Brain Power*, and *1001 Internet Freebies*.

Morgan resides with her husband, daughter, two cats, and dog in historic Hampton Roads, Virginia. Find her online at **www.kimomorgan.com**.

Index

Pole pruner, 53

Pollarding, 99-101, 278

Privet, 217, 223-224, 235, 238

Pruning paints, 71-72

R

Rhododendrons, 256

Root crown, 19, 74, 93-94, 278

Root graft, 80-81, 278

Root pruning, 21, 260, 91-95, 97, 139, 141-142, 279

Rose bushes, 24, 80, 121

Rosemary, 118-119

S

Saws, 39-40, 48, 51, 54-57

Shearing, 44, 51, 90, 112, 220, 224-227, 234, 240-242, 249-250, 260

Shears, 49-52, 54, 59, 65, 77, 81, 89, 128, 131-133, 148-149, 155, 160, 163, 204, 279, 217, 219, 226

Silver leaf, 172, 199

Spruces, 146-148, 240, 244, 246

Suckers, 25, 36, 63, 76, 80-81, 87, 153, 165, 173, 181, 184-185, 188, 190, 192, 195, 197, 199, 210, 212, 214, 254, 258, 260-261, 279

T

Topiary, 122-133, 153, 279-280, 282

Topping, 23, 37, 67, 82, 100, 112, 237, 272

Transpiration, 20-22, 95, 279

U

Unisexual, 186-187

USDA, 23-24, 26-27, 55-56, 71, 110, 114, 226, 228, 230, 265

W

Walnut trees, 209-211

Water sprouts, 36, 63, 80-81, 87, 153, 155, 160, 165, 169, 181, 184-185, 190, 196-197, 199, 261, 279

Whorled buds, 66, 246-247

X

Xylem, 21-22, 274, 279-280

Y

Yews, 129-130, 227, 239-240, 247-248